DIGITAL TRANSFORMATION REQUIRES STRATEGIC DIRECTION

POINTS

A BLUEPRINT FOR DIGITAL MARKETING STRATEGY

Sergio Restrepo

DIGITAL TRANSFORMATION REQUIRES STRATEGIC DIRECTION

POINTS

A BLUEPRINT FOR DIGITAL MARKETING STRATEGY

Sergio Restrepo

ABOUT THE AUTHOR

 Sergio Restrepo is a digital marketing expert who understands how to craft multimarket digital strategies. After twelve years working in digital marketing, Sergio understands just what makes customers tick and that is an authentic and human connection with brands. With a passion for entrepreneurship, Sergio has built businesses around Amazon FBA, Ebay dropshipping, brick and mortar stores, online automobile auctions, e-learning, IOT, CRM system Integration, digital marketing agencies, regulated industries ventures, among others.

He has developed digital marketing strategies in new and existing market territories for dozens of global brands including Nestle, 3M, New Balance, Sab Miller, Honda, and Johnson & Johnson, to mention a few. Sergio is an invited professor at Boston University (USA), ESADE Business School (SPAIN), Georgetown University (USA) and INCAE Business School (Latam). Sergio lives in New York city.

Sergio´s areas of expertise:

- Multi-cultural marketing and diversity
- US Hispanics (e.g., localizing for the US Hispanic market)
- Digital transformation initiatives
- Customer centric marketing / Customer lifecycle engagement design
- Marketing Cloud integrations
- Multimarket Digital Marketing Strategy
- Bootstrap marketing for entrepreneurs

https://www.linkedin.com/in/sergiorestrepoarango/

www.sergiorestrepo.com

TABLE OF CONTENTS

INTRODUCTION

How Did We Get Here...?

It´s not about digital marketing, it´s about marketing in a digital world.

Today, marketing and advertising come at us from every angle. You cannot turn on a television, radio, or computer without seeing or hearing some type of advertisement. They are in the stores we visit, on billboards as we drive down the street, and even on social media, video sites, and plenty of other digital platforms.

Those who want to succeed in marketing and sales today need to know how to create an effective strategy. In addition, they need to embrace technology, as marketing will always follow technology.

Why Is Transparency Important?

Customers today are very smart, and they know how to use the Internet to research items that interest them, including the products you are trying to sell. They can check reviews, look at what the competition is offering, and they can learn the truth about a product with a speed and accuracy that was impossible in the past. The Internet has helped to make a smarter consumer, for the most part. Sure, there are still those who are easily duped, but they are not the majority. Buyers today are savvier than they were in the past.

Because it is easy to do research, estimates are that 70% of the buyer's journey is complete before the customer ever talks to sales. It is impossible to overuse backlinks or stuff keywords today, which means a big part of marketing is creating good and valuable content for the customers. You need to provide them with the truth, and you need to be transparent about the marketing.

When you are transparent about your ads and marketing, as well as about the value the product can provide, it engenders trust with the potential customers. In today's digital age, gaining and keeping this trust is essential. Missteps are going to lose customers, and it will cause your product or company to accumulate bad reviews.

As we mentioned, customers look up reviews before they buy. Bad reviews and dishonest practices mean they will pass you over for the competition. Honesty and transparency is the "new marketing", and it is something you need to embrace sooner rather than later.

Making the Ads Personal

With user-generated content and big data, it is possible to create a personalized experience through marketing.

Big data is fantastic for providing you with the information you need about customers, while user-generated content can help to bring customers "into the fold" so to speak. By allowing users to add some of their own information or experiences via social media or another outlet, it makes them feel closer to the company. It also encourages them to share the content so their friends and family can see it. This provides your company or product with an even bigger audience.

As a marketer, you need to find ways to connect with people in the digital age. You have to build a rapport with them that's not much different from the rapport created between the traveling salespeople of yesterday and their customers.

Evolution in Segmentation

Over the years, marketers have also developed a range of methods for segmenting the market, and it is important to get an idea of what those methods are. There are six basic approaches:

- Mass Marketing
- Product Variety Marketing
- Target Marketing
- Micro Marketing
- Customized Marketing
- Personalized Marketing

Yes, we can still talk about segments, however we are in the constant search for more personal conversations.

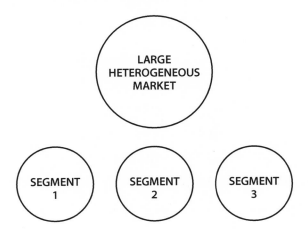

Mass Marketing

Also called undifferentiated marketing, this was the older and traditional approach to marketing. It applied marketing that was the same across the board to all customers without truly thinking about their needs or wants. This sort of marketing does not consider differences such as lifestyle, income, education, or experience. The goal of the marketing program is to appeal to all the various buyers, not just a portion of the audience.

Some companies today still utilize this approach. One of the most famous and successful examples is Coca-Cola. However, this will not work for all companies. Some of the types of products that this can work well for include:

- Stationery items
- Over the counter medication
- Fruits and vegetables
- Sodas and similar drinks

Product Variety Marketing

This type of marketing is also called differentiated marketing. Marketers know that people are not going to accept "standard" products for certain things. For this reason, they introduce features, shapes, colors, sizes, etc. to help attract more customers. By having this variety in their products, it can provide options for a wider range of consumers. You can see this in a variety of products from vehicles to clothing.

Target Marketing

The goal of target marketing is to help marketers identify the right groups of people, or market, for their goods. Target marketing can be extremely beneficial when done properly, and it will typically include three main steps.

In market segmentation, the goal is to provide groups of buyers who might benefit from marketing mixes or separate products. During market targeting, the market segments to enter are chosen. Market positioning then requires the marketer to showcase the benefits for the market provided by the product. They may use a shotgun approach, which requires treating the target as a single aggregate market with a single marketing mix specifically for them. The rifle approach is another option. In those cases, the selection of segments will depend on the company's capabilities.

Micro Marketing

Target marketing is often turning toward micro marketing. This creates even smaller target groups on which the marketers focus, and they are often addressed locally and individually. Often, these niches do not attract competitors, and they are for customers who are willing to pay a premium to have what they want. Even though it might be a niche, it has the capability to grow in both size and profit.

Customized Marketing

Target marketing is becoming more and more customized to the individual. This is possible thanks to improved technology. It is possible to market to people with customized services, which help those individuals see their importance to the company from which they are buying or whose services they are using. This can help to breed customer loyalty, which can help to grow a business and garner more sales. This type of marketing is often used for custom products and services.

Personalized Marketing

While customized marketing utilizes custom products and services, personalizing the marketing messages themselves for other types of companies can help to foster loyalty. According to authors of One Size Fits One, Heil, Parker and Stephens, there are ten rules for building relationships with customers:

1. The average customer does not exist.
2. Make the customer's experience special. Give the customer something to talk about.
3. If something goes wrong, fix it quickly.
4. Guarantee customer satisfaction.
5. Trust the customer and the customer will trust the company.
6. Customers' time is as important as the company.
7. Do not take the customer for granted.
8. The details are important to the customer, as they should be to the company.
9. Employ people who are ready and willing to serve the customer.

10. The customer cares to find out whether company is a responsible corporate system.

You may also notice in your own life that you tend to put more trust in companies that have marketing efforts that seem more personalized. It is a good option, especially in the modern digital world where everyone seems to be invisible.

About POINTS Methodology

In this book, we will be discussing each of the elements in a system we created call the POINTS Methodology. This is a step-by-step blueprint that will help you to build solid, repeatable digital marketing strategies. Once you understand it, POINTS methodology is easy to employ into your marketing system.

Step-by-Step Process

The POINTS Methodology is a step-by-step process that can improve the way companies are currently conducting their digital marketing efforts. It accounts for all of the most important aspects an organization needs to consider during the marketing process.

Why Do So Many Companies Have Trouble?

Digital marketing, on the surface, looks easy enough. It seems as though anyone can just jump in and get started. While it might be easy to set up some social media and buy a few ads, there is a difference between using digital techniques and knowing how to incorporate those techniques into your company for the best results.

Many companies today fail with their digital marketing efforts because they have no strategic maps in place for digital marketing. They are essentially "flying blind" and hoping they find something that works. Instead of having a real plan, they utilize tactical initiatives and believe it is the same thing as strategy. However, it's not. Those are individual tactics and not a full plan, which you need if you hope to succeed.

When the POINTS Methodology is used, it can help to provide companies with the roadmap that is needed to develop a powerful digital marketing strategy that works. Having a plan in place, knowing the steps you need to take, and the tools you need to use, will make successful digital marketing much easier.

It Takes Time

Incorporating a workable and actionable digital marketing strategy is not likely to happen overnight. It takes time and effort, along with a lot of fine tuning before a company can get things just right. In fact, the process can take up to five years of tweaking and tuning your plans to have a great system in place. Even when you have a good system.

Be Digital , Don't Just Do Digital

Many companies are still in the stages of "doing digital" rather than "being digital". It is important to understand what this difference really means.

Those who are "doing" rather than "being" tend to be organizations that realize they need to be working with digital and who may have started to incorporate various digital strategies and technologies, but who have not yet incorporated it into their daily business routines. Those who are becoming digital are consciously and actively incorporating digital into their business so it is a daily part of their company, not just something they do. It can and should be incorporated into all of the organizational goals.

This should be the goal for all businesses out there, and the POINTS Methodology is a huge step in the right direction.

Whether you are just getting into digital marketing for your company, or you have been trying to use digital marketing for years and just can't get it right, start using the techniques and tips found in the POINTS Methodology, as it can make a big difference.

For now, I want to provide you with a very brief rundown of the pieces in the method and let you know what each of the steps and letters stands for before we get started.

- **P** – Stands for several different things – People, Problem, Purpose, and Partners. We will discuss all of these over the course of the book.
- **O** – Objectives
- **I** – Initiatives
- **N** – Numbers
- **T** – Technology
- **S** – Sustainability

That's the basics of what POINTS stands for. As we delve into each of these steps in the following pages, it will all start to make a lot more sense, and you will see how you can start using this methodology for your own marketing. It is a reliable system that can make a real difference in the success of your marketing efforts.

Let's Get Started

Now, it's time that we started to delve deeper into the world of digital marketing. Don't worry; we won't go to the deep end of the pool quite yet. In the first chapter of the book, we'll be covering the fundamentals, as well as the new marketing standard, integrated marketing, strategy, tactics, design thinking basics and more. Then, we will get deeper into what this new marketing world truly means and how you can use digital to your advantage.

CHAPTER 1

Fundamentals

---

*"What people don't realize is that professionals are
sensational because of the fundamentals."*
—*Barry Larkin*

Whether you are brand NEW to marketing, or you have been in the field for decades, it is important to have a solid grasp of the fundamentals. If you are just looking to start directly on your step by step process for POINTS, please jump to chapter 3.

The New Marketing Normal

Is there a new single normal when it comes to marketing? While we have certainly seen trends that have led to new methods of marketing, it is important to remember that there is no single marketing method that is going to be flawless for all the companies out there. After all, every company is different, and so is every product. Even when the products are similar to the competition, the marketing approach taken could be different.

In addition to the traditional 4P model in traditional marketing, we believe it´s time to add:

Participation

Associate participation to user interaction, one to one, one to many or many to many. This is now possible thanks to the social web or what was also called web 2.0 in early stages. Communication is now bidirectional; the power has shifted to the user.

Principles

Principles and values are making a comeback. New generations are demanding their brands of choice to have a clear and compatible work, service and productions ethics. Companies that are not transparent or fail to address and revisit their core purpose, principles and values will have a hard time adapting to the new marketing normal.

4P	5P	6P New Normal
PRODUCT	PRODUCT	PRODUCT
PRICE	PRICE	PRICE
PLACE	PLACE	PLACE
PROMOTION	PROMOTION	PROMOTION
	PARTICIPATION	PARTICIPATION
		PRINCIPLES

Image 1-Source ID: A1

Customer Lifetime Value

CLV, or customer lifetime value, is the measurement of the "total expected revenue from a customer over their entire relationship with a company." Essentially, it is how much a customer will spend on your product or services during their overall experience with your company.

Many companies neglect to measure this, but it has the potential to be quite helpful for businesses. Knowing how much a customer might spend on your services or products can help you to determine your marketing budget and how much you should spend for each user. For example, if you find out that the CLV of your customers is $100, but you are spending $110 to acquire those customers, you would quickly see you have a problem!

Many companies today will segment the CLV and determine not only the overall CLV, but they will break it down to male, female, and other subgroups that might make sense for the firm. This can provide them with more accuracy, and it allows companies to quickly identify the most valuable customers for more targeting and advertising.

Segmentation

Market segmentation helps businesses target the right customers for their products and services. The goal of segmentation is to find the needs and wants of a specific customer group, creating a segment. This gives them insights into the things they can do in order to provide the services and products for the customers in that segment, and it can make marketing to the segment much easier.

Segmentation is important because it considers the differences in customers. After all, not all customers are the same. They can differ when it comes to the benefits they want, the amount they can pay or what they are willing to pay for the service or product, and the amount they want to buy. Some customers might have different times when they can buy, or they might be more willing to buy in different locations. For example, some people like to buy online, while others are only going to want to buy from a physical location.

In addition, segmentation can provide the companies with insight as to how to best reach the customers. What type of media do they use regularly – Internet, magazines, papers, television, radio, etc.? Knowing their preferred type of media can help a company to develop the right marketing tactics. The segmentation strategies tend to fall into one of four categories:

- Behavioral
- Demographic
- Psychographic
- Geographical

It is important even for small companies to begin segmentation. It can increase the competitiveness of your company, help to increase customer retention and loyalty, improve communication, and ultimately, increase the profitability of the company. In addition, it reduces risk and allows for more focused marketing efforts.

Evolution of Marketing Towards Personalization

Over the past several decades we have seen a trend that moves away from traditional marketing of products toward the masses and an increased effort to personalize the marketing and use a laser focus to market to the right people. Most individuals have become savvy since the creation of the Internet, and they know an ad when they see it.

What Is Digital Marketing for Most People?

The average person today has a good idea of what digital marketing is, at least on the surface of things. Most people know when they are looking at an advertisement on the Internet rather than an article. They know the difference between sponsored posts on social networking sites and news articles or posts from their friends. They have a good understanding of email marketing, as well.

However, not everyone is quite so savvy. Some members of the older generation may have difficulty distinguishing between marketing on the Internet and articles, for example. Therefore, it behooves marketers to make sure they are as transparent as possible so they do not run into problems. For most people, digital marketing will fall into several tactical initiatives and categories, including the following:

- Electronic billboards
- Web-based marketing
- Viral marketing
- Audio advertising
- Email advertising

Of course, as marketers, we know that there are quite a few more details and intricacies when it comes to digital marketing. Always keep in mind this book is about strategy first and initiatives second. Even the content that you put on your blog, while not directly selling, is still a form of marketing. The same is true of the posts made to your social networks that are not directly trying to sell a product. They can help you to establish your brand, which can help find customers and keep them. However, many customers do not realize that jumping into initiatives without a clear blueprint can be a waste of time and resource.

What Is Integrated Marketing?

Integrated marketing is a good way to approach communication in marketing. It is also called IMC, or the integrated marketing community. The goal of this type of marketing is to create a unified, quality experience for the customers who are interacting with your business. This type of marketing tries to combine different forms of advertising including:

- Sales promotions
- Direct marketing
- Social media
- Public relations

They do this with various tactics and methods through different media and channels. They have all their marketing activities working together to achieve the same goal. Of course, the amount of effort and money spent in certain areas for marketing can vary based on the effectiveness of that avenue.

What Is Strategy?

INTEGRATED MARKETING STRATEGY

Image 2-Source ID: A2

The goal of marketing strategies and plans is ultimately to help increase sales and to achieve an advantage over the competition that is sustainable, and hopefully, large. Strategy will encompass all the activities in the field of marketing whether they are long or short-term. In this book, we will be using the POINTS Method to develop a sound marketing strategy that will work well in the digital world.

The exact strategy you choose for your company can vary based on your current market share or dominance/influence in the field. For example, there are leaders, followers, challengers, and niche companies, not to mention pioneers in any field. Where you fall into those categories can determine the best way to market, along with the specifics of that field, of course.

What Is Tactic/Initiative?

What are tactics and initiatives?

Marketing tactics are certain types of strategic methods that are used to help promote goods or services. The tactics for marketing refer to the actual practical things that you will do daily, or at least semi-regularly, to help you with the promotions of your product or service.

Some examples of tactics include:

- Social media
- Engaging with followers/fans/customers and potential customers
- Email marketing
- Writing blog posts and creating other content
- Developing focused digital paid advertisements

Of course, these are just some of the tactics that can be used. As you market more, you will discover more options and you will learn to think outside of the box with some of your tactics.

A marketing initiative is a term used to describe the marketing efforts you undergo, including the various tactics that you might be using. However, it is not about individual tactics; rather, it is about how they can work together. For example, certain branding elements or even characters used across marketing campaigns could be part of an initiative. Insurance companies tend to do this with their commercials, and even with their print ads.

Another type of initiative could be a change in what you are currently doing to market, or even a shift in ideas. As you can see, the term is broad, and it can be used to describe a range of things.

It is also important to keep in mind that most of the time, companies are involved in several marketing initiatives at the same time, which utilize tactics and that are part of an overall strategy. Having just a single initiative or tactic is not going to provide you with the results you want.

Design Thinking Basics

Design thinking involves strategies used by creators during their creation and development process. This can be a valuable tool for many who are marketing, as it can help them to learn to think outside the box in a creative and interesting way. In the past, this was used mainly with new product development. However, it is now a major part of business strategy and innovation.

David Kelley pioneered the five-step process for design thinking. Those steps include the following:

- Empathize – Learn about the customers and what they want and need from a product.

- Define – What is the point of view of the customer? This can provide you with even greater insights to what they want.
- Ideate – Brainstorm various solutions for their problems. What does your product do that can help to alleviate those issues?
- Prototype – Show the idea to the users.
- Test – Get feedback from the users who have tested the prototype and then make changes based on that feedback.

As you can see, these steps are ideal for new product development. However, you can also use those same steps when developing a marketing plan. Know more about your customers and what they want; determine the best ways to market to them through various channels, begin the campaign and see how it fares, making changes when needed to focus on the right customers. It's as easy as that.

Agile PM and Rapid Prototyping

Agile PM

Agile PM, or agile project management, is a type of process that is meant to provide your business with speed and maneuverability when it comes to whatever project you might be working on at the time. Many software products are available that can help companies of all types become faster and more agile in their environment. The goal is to improve and speed up the process, all without cutting any corners. Agile PM is typically used in the tech and software fields, but it can be integrated into other types of businesses, as well.

Some of the different software options that could work for your needs include the following:

- ActiveCollab
- Agilo for Scrum
- Pivotal Tracker
- SprintGround
- TargetProcess
- VersionOne

These are just some of the many options available when it comes to this type of software. If you are going to use software to increase the agility of your team, from production to marketing, consider your type of business first. Then look at the features, as well as reviews from a range of software options to find the one that will work best for your needs.

Agility often requires input from your former customers. They can give you an idea of the things you are doing right, and the things that they feel you should or could do better.

Should you pursue this option? The Project Management Institute conducted research and found that those companies that do engage in agile PM tend to fare quite a bit better. Here are some of the results from their research.

- Revenue increased 37% faster
- Agile organizations had 30% more profits
- 67% finished projects on budget – only 45% of non-agile companies finished on budget

- 65% of the projects were finished on time, compared with just 40% of on time projects from non-agile organizations
- 75% of the goals were reached with these companies, whereas only 56% of the goals were reached with non-agile companies

As you can see, the reasons to engage with agile PM are quite compelling. Fortunately, it is not overly difficult to adopt, even for those who are not running a software or tech company. You need to think of agile PM as a mindset rather than a set of digital tools.

You will find that many of the elements that go into this type of management have already been touched upon here. Let's look at the elements you need to keep in mind for this type of management to work.

Know the Problem

Before you can take care of a problem, you have to know what that problem is, naturally. Once you know the problem, you can then start to develop ways to solve the issue.

You will likely have a vision for the finished project. Knowing the goals along the way for the project can give you a better understanding of where the hiccups might be coming from when you run into issues, which can then let you narrow down and isolate where the problem is occurring.

Evolve, Respond, and Adapt

Sometimes, the plan you have to solve a problem might not work very well, or it might not work at all. In those cases, you need to be able to change and evolve your plan to fit the new parameters of your problem. Sometimes, this means going all the way back to the proverbial drawing board. Other times, it might be just a small change here and there.

The important thing is that you are moving quickly and not letting these issues, large or small, linger for too long. After all, you are trying to be agile.

The exact steps to take to adapt your plan and project can vary based on the type of company and where the problem originated. Software has the potential to help you with your efforts here, as it can make setting up an agile PM plan faster and easier.

If you have not adopted this mindset for your company yet, it might be worth considering.

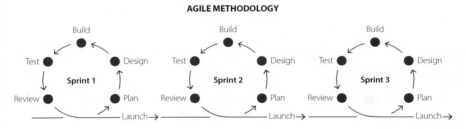

Image 3-Source ID: A3

Rapid Prototyping

Rapid prototyping is a term that is typically used when it comes to manufacturing. It is the creation of a product or a part of a product that can provide a range of benefits for the manufacturers.

- Allows for visualization of the product or part
- Allows testing to make sure the product works properly

- Allows testing of viability and efficiency before mass producing parts
- Can be used to help with the marketing of a product

In marketing, the prototype can be used when writing copy for the marketing, for photos, making videos, and more. This allows for the marketing materials to be created long before the item is mass produced, which lets us get a jump on the marketing. This type of prototyping is often used with automotive parts, as well as software, but it can work with just about any type of product.

Prototyping, for a product or a plan, has four basic steps according to "Rapid Prototyping Methodology in Action: A Developmental Study" by Toni S. Jones and Rita C. Richey. They include:

- Identifying the prototype
- Building the prototype
- Reviewing the prototype
- Freezing the design

The first three elements – identifying, building, and reviewing – can occur time and again, very quickly, until all of the parties are happy with the prototype. At that point, the design is frozen and there are no new features added.

While rapid prototyping can certainly provide you with increased maneuverability and agility, there is the danger that you will never feel as though your design is "complete" and you could keep tinkering. It is important to make sure you have a stopping point.

UX/UI

UX is short for user experience, and UI is short for user interface. Many people conflate the terms and believe that they are interchangeable. While there are some similarities, and you might see some overlap, it is important to realize that these are two very different terms. Both are very important when it comes to a product, and they do work together. It is important to understand what each of them is and how to use them properly.

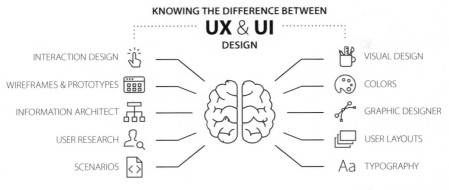

Image 4-Source ID: A4

Understanding User Experience Design

UX is a growing field, and there is still a substantial amount about this subject that is yet to be defined. According to experts in the field and Usability.gov, it is centered around human-computer interaction (HCI) and incorporates a range of disciplines including:

- Project management
- User research
- Usability evaluation

- Information architecture (IA)
- Interaction Design (IxD)
- Visual design
- Content strategy
- Accessibility
- Web analytics

You should think of UX as a human first method of designing products. This pairs well with the new method of marketing, which stresses the human component. Even though you might be marketing a product or service, or even a website, you want to make sure to consider the human element.

The goal is to improve upon the customer's happiness and satisfaction with the product. When you can do this, it helps to increase the loyalty they have for your brand or product. In the 1990s, a cognitive scientist named Don Norman said, "User experience encompasses all aspects of the end-user's interaction with the company, its services, and its products." This, you can see, is a rather broad definition, as it touches upon all contact the person has with your brand.

Therefore, proper UX design is going to look at all of those areas where a consumer might come into contact with the brand. This includes the product, service, your website, social media, marketing, and all other areas that connect with the customers. It can touch on both digital and non-digital, or cognitive areas.

Some of the things you should keep in mind regarding UX include:

- It takes the end user into account
- It can be used before launching a product, and later to improve on that product or service
- It is both a science and an art
- It can be digital and non-digital
- It can increase the value you deliver and the connection a person has with your brand

Why Is UX Important?

Now that you have a better understanding of what UX is, you may still want to know why it is so important. Today, companies realize that having designs centered on the user is essential. As we mentioned, this type of experience can improve the way a customer thinks about your product or service.

If you do not improve your UX, you can be sure that customers are eventually going to move away from you and head to the competition that they feel does care about them and their needs. If the client or customer is not happy, they will stop interacting with you. UX can take care of that problem.

It really is as simple as that.

Understanding User Interface Design

You may have a solid understanding of what UX is now, but you still need to know more about UI. User interface has been around quite a bit longer than user experience, but it can still be difficult to define. UI tends to cover the more physical aspects of a user's experience.

It utilizes and combines three main concept areas:

- Interaction design
- Visual design
- Information architecture

The interface elements for a product, or website for that matter, need to be easily understood and familiar to those who use them. It is important that you remain as consistent as possible when you are making choices in the design and layout of a site, product, or service.

Some of the different types of interface elements include:

- Input controls
- Navigational components
- Informational components
- Containers

Much of the time when talking about the UI elements, we're talking about a company's website. To get a better idea of just what makes for good UI, consider what you are looking for in a webpage. In addition to wanting to have a page that loads fast, you do not want to be staring at the screen confused as to what you should do next.

What Are Good Practices for Interface Design?

If you want to have the best possible interface design for products and websites, it is important to know your customers and users. Just as marketing today deals with the human-to-human connection, the interface also needs to consider the goals, tendencies, and preferences of those who will be utilizing the interface you are creating.

After you know what your user wants and expects, you can then begin to develop a quality interface. Keep the following in mind for your design. The following are elements you always want to keep in mind when you are designing your interface on your blog and sites, as well as apps and other digital offerings from your company.

- **Keep it simple** – The best interfaces tend to be very simple and familiar. In fact, they should be almost invisible to the user without any unneeded elements causing any confusion.

- **The system should inform users** – When someone is using the system, it should be able to let users know about errors, changes in state, location, and more. The UI elements can communicate the status changes, so the users are always informed of what's happening. This can help to reduce confusion as well as frustration.

- **Consistent design** – Keeping common elements and design across the UIs for your business helps the users to acclimate quickly, and it and make using the site more efficient.

- **Easy to read** – One of the other things you will want to remember when creating any type of interface, whether it is a blog, a website, or an advertisement is your typography. The fonts you use need to be very easy to read, and they need to be scannable.

- **Consider location of the elements** – The elements on the interface should be easy to find and they should be easy to differentiate from one another. The user should never have to struggle to find what they need.

- **Color and texture can be used tactically** - Consider the colors and textures you are using for your user interface. Not only can you brand with the colors, but you can use different colors and textures as a way to draw the users' eyes toward different areas of the site you want to highlight.

In the past, many individuals and companies made egregious errors on their webpages. Unfortunately, some still do, and it is causing problems with both the UI and the UX. Pages that automatically load music and photo galleries tend to be annoying, especially if there is not a clear and easy way to turn them off. Flash and other flashy graphics and intros can be a real turnoff, as well.

When you are creating the user interface, you can also incorporate some elements of UX into the process. Make sure the interface you design is created with your customers and clients firmly in mind.

When you have a great user interface, and you have considered the user experience to provide the best for your customers, it allows them to get to your content and your offers faster, which is exactly what you want.

Transcreation – Language Localization

If you are in marketing and advertising, you are very likely quite familiar with transcreation. For those who may not be in the know, transcreation is a term that refers to taking a message that is in one language and then adapting it to another language, while keeping the context, tone, style, and intent. It was initially used in the 60s and 70s when referring to ad copy that needed to be put into another language. It has evolved, but it essentially does the same thing today, albeit in the digital world, as well.

THE SPECTRUM OF MARKETING TRANSLATION

	MACHINE TRANSLATION	TRANSLATION	MARKETING LOCALIZATION	TRANSCREATION	BACK TRANSLATION	COPYWRITING
PURPOSE	Just Real-time	Factual	Persuasive	Motivational	Comprehension	Original
ADHERENCE TO SOURCE	Literal	Accurate	Faithful	Conceptual	Conceptual	Authentic
STAKEHOLDER ENGAGEMENT	Very Low	Low	Medium	High	High	Very High
EXAMPLE ASSETS	Business Intel Chat User Gen Cont	Owner Guides Product Specs Press Releases	Websites Campaigns Banners Product Sheets	Email Campaigns Brand Magazines Brochures Headlines	Regulatory Transceated Copy	Magazines Web Content Email Campaigns

Image 5-Source ID: A5

Is It the Same as Translation?

When you first look at the term, you might be thinking to yourself that transcreation is another needless marketing word since it means the same thing as translation. At first blush this might seem to be the case. However, that's not entirely true. There is a difference, even though they are related.

Translation tends to be word-for-word carryover from one language to another and due to idiom and usage differences, this does not work very well at all. A direct translation of something form one language to another often sounds… silly at best and offensive or unintelligible at worst. Good translation considers things such as:

- Idiom
- Grammar
- Syntax
- Vocabulary
- Local usage

It will think about how the target audience to make sure it will make sense to the person who reads it. Transcreation will take things a step further. Instead of merely focusing on the literal text of the piece, it also considers the emotional response of the viewers in the area. It takes the concept in one language and remakes it in another language, which often helps to make it more powerful than mere translation.

Why is this so important? We'll say it again. It's all about the customer. You want the customer to be happy and engaged, and creating marketing that actually speaks to the customer in this way can make them more inclined to buy from you.

If you do not have the capability to do this on your own, and to be honest most companies do not, you will want to work with a transcreation agency that can help. These agencies can help with the marketing and copyrighting to make sure your message is received the way it should be received no matter where you happen to be selling in the world.

GALA, the Globalization & Localization Association provided tips on transcreation that companies can use to get a better handle on this aspect of marketing.

- **Consider if it is really needed** – Are you ready to start selling to other markets around the world, and are you selling in areas that would benefit from marketing plans that have gone through transcreation?

- **Cultural consultation** – Always make sure there has been full cultural testing and consideration to make sure nothing taboo in that culture slips into the marketing.

- **Assets** – Make sure you understand all of the different media platforms you will be using for marketing and advertising in those countries and be sure to put proper transcreation efforts into each of them.

- **Target audience** – Consider the target audience when choosing the language and any country specific slang that you might be using.

- **Tone** – Make sure the tone is right for the country, as well. In some places, sounding too confident can seem boastful and it can be looked down on. Understanding the culture will help with this, as well.

- **Visuals** –the picture and the text need to work with one another in all forms of advertising. When a piece has undergone transcreation, you need to make sure that the image still matches. If it does not, you will need to replace it with something that does.

- **Briefing** – You will need to provide a brief to the copywriters who will be doing the job. Make sure that you have considered all of the elements we've discussed thus far.

- **In-Market Copywriters** – Since language and slang are always changing, you will find that having copywriters who are in the market where you are trying to sell is typically the best option.

- **Time** – Even though we all know that time is of the essence, you do not want to rush when you are trying to create your ads in another language. Rushing could mean putting out something that is not ready and that has problems you should have caught. It's okay to take a little more time to make certain everything has gone through quality control.

- **Debrief** – You will need to explain the importance of transcreation to the owners of your company, or to your clients if you are marketing on your own. They need to know what language barriers and potential cultural issues might be present. It also lets them know why things might take a little longer when working in other languages.

Avoid Problems Marketing Across Cultures

Transcreation was developed because there was the well-founded fear of not being able to reach audiences in other countries. There is a minefield of problems that can arise from poor translations, so you never merely want to run text through a digital translator and think it is good to go. You need proper transcreation to avoid the most common pitfalls of marketing to other cultures.

Culture

How well do you know the culture in a place such as the United Arab Emirates, South Korea, or Brazil? Even though there are similarities to your own country, there are certainly going to be some differences, as well. You do not want your marketing materials to inadvertently offend an entire nation!

Word Use

Word usage is often different, as well. Some words in another language might be very similar, and you could use the wrong words, which make the message difficult to decipher or even unintentionally humorous.

An example that's often discussed when it comes to word usage was when the Honda Fit was trying to market their vehicle in countries in Scandinavia. They used the word "fitta", which happens to be a vulgar world in certain Nordic languages. They had to rename their vehicle – they called it the Honda Jazz – so they could continue marketing in those countries.

Slogans and Puns

If you have a catchy slogan or pun that you use for your company, you should be aware that the translation might not have the same meaning in other countries. Transcreation can certainly help with this respect, but it might not have the same "punch" that it does in your native language.

Research Online, Purchase Offline (ROPO)

When most people think about ecommerce, they imagine a person sitting down on their computer, their tablet or their smartphone, researching a product they want to buy and then hitting the order button online to have it delivered right to their home. While it is true that this is a very common method of buying today – just look at the success of Amazon – it is important to realize that this is certainly not the only way people are buying.

They are also engaging in ROPO, or research online, purchase offline. In fact, according to RetailDive.com, more than 65% of buyers use online product research before they step into a retail store. This means your digital content needs to be on point.

Customers today have a wealth of easy to use tools right at their disposal when it comes to researching items online. They can find digital content about the products, prices, reviews, photos, videos, and even items from the competitors that might interest them just as much as your products. They use search engines, social networks, blogs, and even other online sellers to learn about products that interest them. A survey from KPMG found that the two online channels where they focus the most are the company websites and reviews.

However, they choose not to buy online. Perhaps they want instant gratification and do not want to wait a day or two for Amazon to ship to them. They want to run right out and make their purchase now. That's great, and it can mean more business for your brick and mortar store.

However, you must make sure you are doing everything in your power to leverage the online digital content you are creating. You want those customers to find the information that you are putting out there, so they will then come into your store.

Knowing just how important the information on your website is to the ROPO customers, you need to ensure your content is accurate, descriptive, and that it provides customers with a great overview of what you have to offer and how it can help them. Of course, you also need to work in all of those SEO elements to the content that we've discussed. You also need to make sure you are keeping your customers happy so you can continue to cultivate great reviews.

One of the methods you might want to use to help get more people to come into the store after they have researched your company and products online is offering some type of a discount. Having a coupon that they can print out or show you on their phone for a discount can help people make the decision to buy from you rather than the competition.

Beyond the Basics

Now that we've completed the chapter on some of the fundamentals of marketing, it is time to move forward and start learning more about marketing in the digital world. In the following chapter, we will be learning even more about how the digital age has transformed the way people consume information and the way we market to them.

CHAPTER 2

Digital Transformation

"We've moved from digital products and infrastructure to digital distribution and Web strategy to now into more holistic transformations that clearly are based on mobile, social media, digitization and the power of analytics and we think it's really a new era requiring new strategies."

— *Saul Berman, IBM*

There is no doubt that we are living firmly in the digital age. Most people have access to the Internet, even if they do not own a computer. The web is everywhere, and digital marketing has followed closely behind.

Digital Transformation

Digital transformation is changing the way that many companies do business at all levels, and that includes marketing. The term itself can apply to many things, including changes in the website to be mobile friendly to creating a social media plan.

Those who have not kept up with the digital changes are at a severe disadvantage to those who have embraced digital. In fact, some companies have discovered they need to utilize external experts to help with some of the digital aspects of their business, including marketing.

It is therefore important to try to get everyone in your company on board with the digital transformation as soon as possible. It is essentially a business transformation. It does not mean the traditional methods are all going out the door. It simply means you need to adapt and add digital methods to the things you are doing, as well.

In addition to getting senior leaders and upper management on board with the digital transformation, you must realize it will require a culture change throughout the company. Help people to learn to work with the new technology.

Consider the fact that technology is important to customers, and they are the ones who are adopting new tech and driving the changes in business. You want to keep those customers happy, and you want to make sure those customers are able to visit your site and receive your marketing messages. The only way to do this is by using that technology to your advantage. Many companies today are focusing on their customer's online journey and striving to make it as good as possible for them. Along the way, they are learning more about their customers through things such as data analytics, and this allows them the ability to personalize the customer experience and to make it better overall.

One of the important takeaways from the idea of digital transformation is that it is not a "one and done" change for your company. There will always be new technologies developed. You must make sure you stay abreast of these changes.

Digital Change Drivers

We've seen many changes over the course of the last few years thanks to digital. The behavior of customers is changing, and the subsequent need for marketing changes. However, you might be wondering just what drives digital change? There is no single element. It is a combination of many different forces that have helped to bring about the massive digital changes we've seen.

The following are some of the most prominent drivers to digital change:

- Cloud services
- Automation of processes and businesses
- Increased digital competition
- Increased demands
- Global IT services
- Proliferation of mobile devices
- Widespread use of the Internet
- Increased security demands
- Digital innovation

These are some of the biggest digital change drivers. Some companies may have other prominent drivers that have pushed their customers, and ultimately them, towards the digital space.

3 Steps to Lasting Digital Transformation

When a company knows they need to transform from analog to digital, it can be worrisome. Many companies think it will be too difficult or that the changes will be too great. They worry that the employees will not embrace digital and that they will slip into their old habits, or that they simply will not want to learn how to do things differently. Get those negative thoughts out of your mind. Your company can transform.

It is important to remember that true digital transformation is more than just creating a digital infrastructure. It is about reaching out to digital customers and finding them on the Internet through your website and blog, social media, and through your advertising. It is about learning more about your customers through analytics and about connecting with the customers online.

In marketing, you need to go where the customers are if you hope to make sales. Today, the customers are spending a lot of time in the digital world, and that's what you need to do, as well.

Here are three simple steps that will help your company reach the digital transformation it desperately needs. Best of all, when implemented properly, the changes will last.

Step 1: Make People Aware of the Problem

Change needs to start with awareness. People at the company, from the top to bottom, need to know there is an issue that needs addressing. They need to know how not embracing the digital world is hurting the company and the benefits that going digital in different areas can offer. You can start by speaking with the leadership in the company. Once they are on board, the rest of the management will follow, as well the other employees.

Step 2: Have a Learning Process in Place

For some people, going digital is going to be a big change. You need to make sure the individuals who will now be working in the digital field have the training and resources they need. Look at the key performance indicators or KPI of the individuals and teams at the company and make sure they change and are in line with the company after the digital transformation.

Step 3: Encourage Digital

Once you undergo a digital transformation, you can't look backwards. You need to continue working in the digital realm. Encourage people and reward people who are working in the digital field at your company. Some companies, for example, have promoted digital designers and digital marketers to CEOs. This helps to underscore how important they are.

Mastery: Model, Immersion, Spaced Repetition

How should you go about trying to master digital marketing? It's just like anything else that you might want to attempt to master, really, and Tony Robbins has illustrated three main points when it comes to achieving mastery. They include:

- Model
- Total Immersion
- Spaced Repetition

Find a Model

You will want to find someone in the field who is outstanding and that you want to emulate. They should be someone who has achieved the things that you hope to achieve on multiple occasions. They need to be a true expert. Once you find this person, you will want to model yourself after them. This can help to accelerate the learning time, and it can make understanding how to market faster and easier.

As mentioned, this is a good tip not only for digital marketing, but for anything you might like to master.

Total Immersion

If you want to be the best at marketing in the digital world, or anything else, you need to fully immerse yourself in the field. You can't dabble here and there and expect to become an expert. It doesn't work like that. Total immersion is the best option, but keep in mind this doesn't mean you never take a break, as you will see from the next section.

Spaced Repetition

You do not want to burn out, and you do not want to become frustrated. Sometimes, it is smart to walk away from something and then come back to it. When you are constantly involved with trying to learn something, it can cause you to lose perspective. Take a break and come back refreshed. While you were away, you might have even discovered that your mind helped work on your problems on a subconscious level.

CHAPTER 3

POINTS Methodology starts with - People

"Get closer than ever to your customers. So close that you tell them what they need well before they realize it themselves." –Steve Jobs

N ow, we've moved on to the chapters that describe the POINTS Method. Here, we will be discussing the aspect of "people" when it comes to digital marketing. There is quite a bit more happening than some marketers assume.

POINTS METHODOLOGY / DIGITAL MARKETING BLUE PRINT

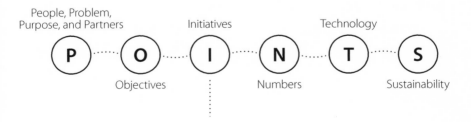

People, Problem, Purpose, and Partners — P   Initiatives — I   Technology — T

Objectives — O   Numbers — N   Sustainability — S

B2B vs. B2C vs. H2H

Anyone who has been involved in marketing for any length of time knows the terms B2B as business to business and B2C as business to customer. This is one of the most common segmentations in marketing, and each has their own audiences and requirements when it comes to marketing. Over time, the lines have become blurred though.

Many also feel this way of marketing led to unnatural language and jargon that has crept into the field… and it's true. By now, people are very tired of hearing the word synergy.

Consumers want things to be simple, and that's what marketers should strive for when they are attempting to connect with people. Think like the consumers and learn what they want. Put yourself firmly in the buyer's mindset and speak to the customer. Find the solutions the customers want, let them know about it in simple language, and make the entire process, including buying the product or service, as simple as possible.

H2H

A business cannot engage with a person one-on-one… a marketer can. The marketers should work to connect with people on a human level. As Bryan Kramer says, this is becoming known as H2H, or human to human, marketing. Make it simple and connect. It holds a substantial amount of potential when it comes to marketing now and in the future.

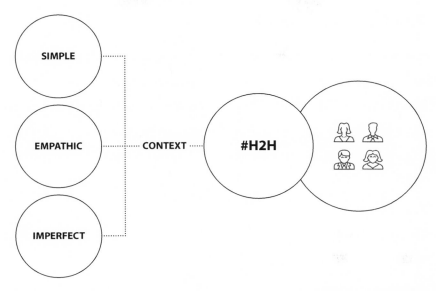

Image 6-Source ID: A6

Empathy

Since we now know that we want to market in the digital world with an eye on human to human contact, it becomes very important to understand how human beings work, and how they engage with various technologies.

One of the biggest areas to consider is empathy. It is essential for marketers to be aware of and empathetic of the goals of their potential customers, whatever they might be. Having empathy toward your fellow humans helps to form a bond with them; and this is essential for HCM, or human centered marketing. You are going beyond just the digital technologies to reach out to someone. You are trying to establish a true connection with the customers, which can help to make them loyal to you.

What Does Empathizing Mean

For most people, empathy is relatively easy when it comes to face-to-face communications. Of course, now marketers are often only connected to customers digitally. In today's world, marketers need to think about how they can remain empathetic when engaging with people in the digital world.

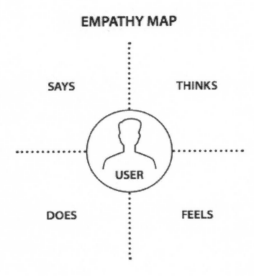

Image 7-Source ID: A7

There are several things marketers can and should do if they want to empathetically connect with people, digitally or otherwise. Learn to experience the world through the eyes of the consumer. How do they see and use the Internet? Observe the human and physical context in which people are working and living in today. In addition, you need to listen to what the buyers and prospective customers are saying.

Qualitative interviews can be helpful in this regard, as they can provide a better and deeper communication regarding peoples' experiences, emotions, activities, and identities.

Interaction with the customers is important, too. For companies and marketing teams, interaction is possible through their own website and blog, as well as through social media outlets. It is important to do more than just set up those accounts. They need to make the effort to connect with the customers there. Remember, this is the new world of human-to-human marketing.

It is unfortunate, but empathy is far rarer today in the digital world. Many feel the world is becoming a colder and shallower place because of it. By showing true empathy, it does allow marketers to connect better with their potential customers.

It is possible for marketers to learn through empathy. They can learn to design content that is better suited to their customers. They can focus on the things that truly matter to the customers they have and the types of customers they hope to reach. Improving empathy is something all marketers should strive to achieve.

Values Marketing

The goal of values marketing is to appeal to the ethics or values of a customer. As you know, in the past, a substantial amount of marketing was focused on the product rather than the customer. Values marketing changes the focus and centers more on the customer, and it is a powerful way to leverage their emotions.

Forming a values-based connection with the audience can improve the loyalty of the customers and even create advocates for the brand. More and more shoppers today are looking for a connection with the companies they choose, and they want to develop a relationship with the brands.

Let's get a better look at the basic goals that stem from values marketing. They can be placed into four basic elements.

- Focus on the customer
- Be socially responsible
- Create business alliances
- Consider customer values

Focus on the Customer

Values marketing needs to be aware of what the customer base, and what the society in general, think about certain topics. Here is a simple example.

In recent years, there has been quite a bit of pushback against companies that manufacture junk food aimed at children. People have come to understand just how much of a problem this sort of food can be. By showing that a company values the health of children, just like the parents, and that they are providing a healthy option for the children, it can appeal to the values of those parents. This can make them more likely to buy the products.

Be Socially Responsible

Social and economic responsibility is more important to the audience of today than it has been in a long time. Therefore, it makes sense for any type of values based marketing to look at the social and economic problems of the day and to ensure that their own corporate practices are not a part of the problem. Companies that admit that they may have a problem in one of these areas, and that strives to fix that issue in a public venue, can garner support from many. This does not mean that all those who support the company's efforts are going to become customers though.

It is important to make sure the values your company espouses in marketing messages and on social media is what your brand truly believes. If you are merely trying to "cash in on" a movement, it will be easy to spot, and it will not sit well with your potential customers.

Create Business Alliances

While this is not always necessary, it is possible to create alliances with other businesses to achieve the values-based objectives of your company. Consider some other companies in fields that could somehow partner with your business. A food brand, such as a restaurant, might donate time, money, or food to a local shelter, for example. You are doing good for the community, and you are showing the public your values, which can help to engender more trust and loyalty.

Consider the Customer Values

Of course, the most important part of values marketing is understanding just what the customer values are, and both qualitative and quantitative data can help with this. Listen to what your customers are saying on your site and on your social media pages. Understand the overall climate when it comes to different issues, and try to align your values and your customers' values as best you can.

Keep in mind that values can change over time, and as mentioned, you will want to make sure that your brands values are authentic.

This type of values marketing can work with other things as well, of course. It is important to make sure that you have the right marketing message through all your marketing channels, including social media. After all, social media is likely where the people are most likely to interact with your company.

Is Values Marketing for Everyone?

While it is true that values marketing can be very beneficial to the marketer, there are many who believe marketers still need to be carefully. Dr. Carmen Simon, a cognitive neuroscientist, believes that marketers need to be careful when they are choosing specific value types, according to an article on Marketing Dive. Simon also said that peoples' brains are wired for rewards, so it becomes important for companies to understand the need for rewards and motivation.

Another thing to consider when you are engaging in values marketing is that values have the potential to be polarizing. Some people do not have the same beliefs and values as others, and when your company comes out on one side of an issue, it could alienate a certain segment of the audience.

It can also be difficult to change peoples' habits once they have been instilled, and this is always going to be a challenge for marketers. Values marketing could help with this, at least in the case of some consumers. It is certainly worth considering, and it does tie in nicely with the "People" portion of the POINTS system.

Buyer Personas

Developing a buyer persona can help you to understand what customers and prospective customers are thinking when they are considering the products or services your company sells. It can provide you with insight as to the decision-making process of the customers when they are deciding how your company can resolve the problems they have... or if your company is even the right solution for them.

The buyer persona is an in-depth profile of the buyer, as it can provide you with a look at the actual decision-making process, not merely the outcome. It is more than just the overview of the buyer.

Understanding how your customers and potential customers think can help the marketing team. They can focus their efforts on those areas. When you understand how to help the buyers on their own terms as they are evaluating your offerings, it allows you to build a conversation with the customer, as well as trust.

Things to Consider When Developing Buyer Personas

What priorities do the customers have when they are looking for solutions offered by companies such as yours? Why do some of the buyers invest? What is it that makes them spend their time and money on certain items? What about those buyers who are fine with whatever the status quo might be?

What results does the subject of the buyer persona expect when they choose a solution? Is your product or service capable of living up to or exceeding those expectations?

Look at your company's offerings. Are there any elements that might cause a buyer to believe that your company's options are not the best solution? If so, make sure you understand what they are and what you can do to minimize or eliminate them entirely. Many times, the customer's perceptions are tied to previous negative experiences they have had with similar solutions.

© marketoonist.com

Tips for Developing Buyer Personas

When you are developing your buyer personas, you can follow a few simple rules to help you develop better, more accurate buying insights.

First, if your buyer does not say it matters, then it is not something that should go into the buyer persona. Just because you believe it matters does not mean it makes any difference to the buyers. Second, one of the best ways to develop buyer personas is to interview people who have bought from you recently. Their decisions to buy are likely fresh in their mind, which means their insights should be more accurate and more helpful.

Keep in mind that the buyer personas should be segmented only on how and why people buy. They should not be based on all the different product lines and options you offer. Quite often, less is more when it comes to developing a buyer persona.

When interviewing to develop a buyer persona, it is a bad idea to work from a script. Speak with the customer on a human-to-human level and listen to the answers they give you. When you are actively listening, and engaging with the buyer, they are often more willing to share more information and provide you with better info for your buyer personas.

A buyer persona provides the details regarding who and what are important in the buying decision from the buyer's point of view. It takes out the guesswork, which is often wrong. You will have a firm understanding of the things your buyers perceive as being the most important or critical. You can then focus marketing efforts for those people and alleviate their worries about those critical areas.

Customer Centric Marketing

Customer centric marketing is a type of strategy where the customer is the central focus of the marketing strategy and the team's delivery plan. The most important thing to take away from the idea of customer centric marketing is to eliminate the idea of the "average" customer. All customers will have different types of behaviors. They will have different preferences, as well.

	Customer Value	Personalization	Proposition	Use of Data/Insights	Media Channels/ Mix	Voice
BRAND CENTRIC APPROACH	Customers I **DON'T** have matter most	Customers who may be like you	What's **HOT**	Here 's something I **COULD** offer	The Coolest / Newest / Cheapest	Sell, sell, sell, sell ... and, **YOU'RE WELCOME**
CUSTOMER CENTRIC APPROACH	Customers I **DO** have matter most	You	What your data says you might want or need	Here 's something I **SHOULD** offer	What's most effective for each customer	Recommend, invite, help, sell and **THANK YOU**

Image 8-Source ID: A8

Older marketing concepts, which had a one plan for everyone or a one size fits all approach are simply not working any longer. This customer centric approach changes the focus of the marketers.

What is the best long-term investment for your company? It's your customers, naturally. By placing this focus on your customers at every level in the company, it can help to ensure a stronger bond between the customer and the company as well as better marketing.

Because you are focusing on the customers with this type of marketing, rather than the product, the channel, or an event, you have a better understanding of what they want. This works well with values marketing and the development of buyer personas. The marketing team can target the customer with the best channel and message, and it can reach them at the right time.

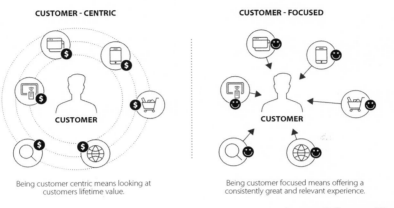

Image 9-Source ID: A9

This type of marketing can encourage customers to keep coming back time and again, and it makes it easier to acquire high-value customers.

In addition to loyalty, this type of marketing has proven to be quite efficient. There is less wasted time and effort. Because you can engage with customers at the right time, it also provides the marketers with more agility than other marketing methods, such as product centric marketing.

Instead of using generic offers, you are using offers directed at individual customers who are more inclined to buy from you and who are more likely to become advocates for your brand. Using customer centric marketing gives you a unified view of the customer across channels.

Start Using Customer Centric Marketing

If you are not already engaged in this type of marketing, you should roll this into your marketing plan. You will understand your customers better, acquire better customers, driver more repeat business, and retain those customers you have worked so hard to find.

CUSTOMER-CENTRIC JOURNEY

4 **INSPIRED** by Customers

3 **ENGAGED** with Customers

2 **RESPONSIVE** to Customers

1 **TARGETED** on Customers

Image 10-Source ID: A10

Customer Journey

The customer journey is important to understand for any marketer. It is the journey, from start to finish, that any buyer makes when purchasing a product or service. This journey can be broken down into three to even seven basic phases that applies to all customers regardless of what they are buying. Understanding the customer journey helps to make things easier when it comes to implementing the other techniques that we've talked about in this chapter.

The following are the phases of the customer journey:

| AWARENESS | CONSIDERATION | PURCHASE/ ACTION | RETENTION | ADVOCACY |

Image 11-Source ID: A11

Discovery or Awareness Phase

The discovery phase of the consumer's journey occurs as soon as they begin to search for products or services related to what you offer. In fact, the first place that the customer journey for your items will take place is in the search engines. Therefore, you can understand just why it is so important to make sure you have quality online content and great search engine rankings for your product or service. You want to be one of the first places the customer visits, and you want to be sure the information that comes up regarding your offerings paints you in a great light.

Optimizing your search with SEO techniques and buying ads for the search terms your buyers will be using is essential. It means those customers will find your company during the discovery phase of the consumer's journey. Chances are you will have more than one link on the first page of results, so long as you have built a strong web presence.

One of the things to keep in mind about this, however, is that with multiple links showing up in the search results, it means there are

51

multiple avenues through which the customer can continue their journey with you. For example, an advertisement might lead to a purchase page or product page, whereas a blog post about your company might lead to your blog instead.

No matter where your customer ends up, you want to make it as easy as possible for them to buy from you when they have made their decision. Once they have found your company, they begin the second phase of the customer journey.

Consideration and Shopping

It is also important to understand the zero moment of truth, or ZMOT. The Internet has changed the way people buy things and how people decide exactly what it is they are going to buy. This is called the ZMOT, and it refers to the moment of the buying process when the consumer researches a product prior to purchasing it.

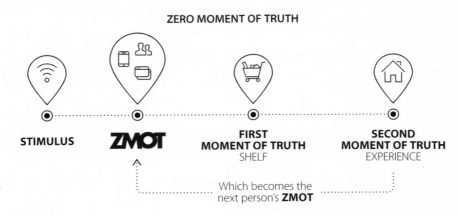

Image 12-Source ID: A12

Once the customer has a good idea of what they want based on their research, they continue shopping for the right product. Ideally, they will click on your ads or your website and arrive at a landing page that helps to guide them through the rest of the process. The landing page for customers should be a product page or a product category page.

Keep in mind that the customer is not likely only looking at one option for their needs. Whether they are looking for a service, such as a dentist or a gym, or they are looking for an electronic device, or anything else for that matter, they are going to look at what the competition offers.

During the shopping part of their journey, make sure they see your product as the better option out of the others on the market. You may market with an eye toward showing your products or services as a better value because of quality or because of price.

Remember, you need to think about what the customer wants and what they are expecting when you are marketing, as these things will be in their mind during their shopping phase. They are often looking for information about your product or service that will educate them and let them know more about why your company is the best choice.

Purchasing or Taking an Action of Some Type

This is considered to be the first moment of truth in the consumer's journey, and ideally, it is one that all your potential customers will reach. They will make their purchase of your goods or service. They have already made their decision, and little stands in the way of the sale now. However, if they are buying directly from your site, as often happens in the digital age, you need to make sure the checkout process is as seamless and secure as possible.

People are not willing to give up their credit card number unless you can assure them that your site is secure. You should make the entire checkout process as fast and easy as possible, too.

It is also during this stage that you can introduce upsells, as well as promotions. Keep in mind that this is not something all consumers want to see. If you have feedback from a large number of customers that say they would rather not have you trying to upsell in the checkout, it might be something you will want to reconsider.

Make sure that you are looking at your analytics to learn more about your customer demographics and their behavior on your site. If you are not getting customers through the checkout process and they are abandoning their carts, this is information you need. It can help you alter your marketing and sales plan to reduce the number of shopping cart abandonments.

If you hope to have a successful ecommerce business, you need to understand the customer journey. You also need to realize that the journey can differ somewhat from one customer to another. Combine your knowledge of the customer journey with the other elements we've discussed in this chapter, and you will have a much better grasp of the "People" portion of this method.

Retention

Retention can be considered the second moment of truth, as can advocacy. The retention phase of the customer journey is simply, but it is important. This means that the brand has a good enough product, program, or service that the customer who bought from them decides that he or she will contain to do business with them. This is the start of someone becoming a truly loyal customer.

Of course, as a business, you should strive to take steps that will help to retain the customers. Provide great customer care and service, provide them with discounts on future purchases, and take other steps that help to keep your company in the good graces of your consumers.

Advocacy

An advocate is one of the most powerful allies you can have. They tell their family and friends about your company and what you can offer, and many will even post online reviews about the product or service. When someone advocates for a brand or product, their advocacy has the potential to become another customer's zero moment of truth, which helps to complete the cycle.

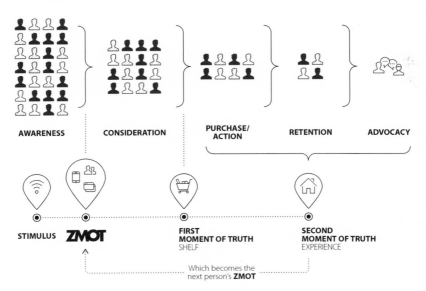

Image 13-Source ID: A13

Is the Customer Lifecycle the Same as the Customer Journey?

You may hear people using the terms customer journey and customer lifecycle interchangeably. However, they are not the same, and it is important that you know the difference between them.

FIVE INSIGHTS INTO A BUYING DECISION...

	BUYERS TELL US	SO YOU CAN CHOOSE
Priority Initiative	Who triggers the search and why	Targeting and messaging for demand generation campaigns
Success Factors	What outcomes buyers expect in their own words	The benefits you will emphasize to position your solution as an exact fit
Perceived Barriers	Why this buyer wouldn't make this decision or choose you	What you will say and do to overcome barriers to consideration or purchase
Decision Criteria	Which capabilities or attributes this buyer evaluates	How you will give buyers the useful information that helps them decide
Buyers Journey	Which buyers are involved and how they weigh options to choose one	How and when you will deliver your message and to which audiences

Customer Journey

From the last section, you should have a good understanding of what the customer journey is. It divides the buyer's experience into several phases including discovery, consideration, purchasing, retention, and advocacy. The customer journey can take varying amounts of time. With some customers and some types of businesses, it might take only a few minutes to go through the journey. Other times, it could take months.

A marketer should strive to provide a great experience through each step of the customer journey. The experience you provide can be enhanced by all the other tools and techniques that we discuss in this book, such as content and social media outlets. For some, the definition of customer journey includes a buyer's interaction with a brand at every level. It could include the content you create, word of mouth advocacy from friends or family, and all other interactions that customer has with your brand.

© marketoonist.com

Customer Lifecycle

The customer lifecycle, also called the buyer lifecycle, may seem to have similarities to the customer journey, but there are some important differences. By segmenting the potential customers into stages, it will make it easier for you to alter your marketing and sales to help improve your conversion rate. These stages are what helps to create your marketing sales funnel. When customers pass through the different stages, they are moving close to becoming an actual customer.

As happens with marketing funnels, there will be fewer and fewer customers who pass through the various layers of the funnel. Even though there will be fewer potential customers, they are quality. There is a better chance that they will complete the lifecycle and become buyers and eventually evangelists.

There are seven stages to the customer lifecycle. They include:

- **Subscriber** – Someone who has at least a casual interest to the content you provide
- **Lead** – A person who has provided you with information about themselves, perhaps by signing up for a newsletter or completing a survey
- **Marketing qualified lead (MQL)** – The leads that fall into this category are ready to receive marketing messages
- **Sales qualified lead (SQL)** – These leads are ready to receive sales messages
- **Opportunity** – At this stage, the potential customer is ready to buy, and they are receiving sales correspondence
- **Customer** – As the name suggests, this is someone who has purchased your product or service
- **Evangelist** – A customer is happy with your product or service, and they are advocating for your brand

Image 14-Source ID: A14

The marketing team needs to make sure they have a clear definition for these stages. However, they are unique to each company, so there are no "standard" rules that you can follow. Still, there are some best practices you can keep in mind. You should always provide quality content, special offers, and work to nurture the customer. You may even want to include sales follow-ups. Your goal as a marketer is to make the customer journey and the customer lifecycle work seamlessly together.

Net Promoter Score, or NPS

Net Promotor Score is a types of management tool that can be quite helpful for those who need to determine the loyalty of their customer relationships. While some companies are utilizing the usual customer satisfaction methods to learn more about how their customers feel about the company, more and more companies are starting to adopt the NPS method.

NPS as a loyalty metric was developed by Fred Reichheld, Bain & Company, and Satmetrix Systems. Reichheld introduced the idea in an article called "One Number You Need to Grow", which was published in the Harvard Business Review.

The NPS can range from -100 to +100. At -100, it would mean that everyone who says something about the brand is a detractor and most definitely not a fan. Those who are at +100 means just the opposite – everyone is a fan and promoter of the brand.

Of course, it is unrealistic for any company, no matter how beloved they might think they are, to have a score of +100. The same is true for -100. Most companies will fall from 0 to +50. Those who have a score above 0 are said to have a good score, and those who are doing exceptionally well might have a score of +50.

A Simple System

One of the reasons this is a popular option is because it is relatively easy to utilize. It is based on just one question. You have probably seen and responded to this question before for other brands. It is simply "How likely is it that you would recommend our company/product/service to a friend or colleague."The scoring system for the question is generally a scale that goes from 0 to 10.

Here's how the scoring breaks down for this system:

- Responders who choose 0 through 6 are considered detractors
- Responders who choose 7 or 8 are considered passive
- Responders who choose 9 or 10 are considered promoters

To calculated the score for the NPS, you would subtract the percentage of detractors from the percentage of promoters. Passive respondents count toward the total number of responders, which will then decrease the percentage of both promoters and detractors. This will push the score toward 0.

As you can see, those who have a score higher than 0 are doing well. Of course, the higher the better. By improving every step of the customer journey and their interactions with your company, this is possible. You can take the data that you receive and then get an idea of why they might not be promoters of your company. You can look at ways to improve. It might take some time to increase your NPS, along with hard work, but it can be a good way to get a metric on just how you are doing.

Some of the companies that have started to utilize this approach include:

- Siemens
- Philips
- GE
- Apple Retail
- American Express
- Intuit

Companies often use this to measure loyalty for online applications, as well as games.

The survey may also allow the customer to leave comments, such as why they gave the brand a certain score. The real gold of this system can lie within those comments. The raw scores give you an idea of how you are doing, but it is the information the customer provides in the comments that can help you learn what you need to do to improve your company.

Of course, there are some who believe that the NPS is not the be all end all when it comes to gauging customer loyalty. Some of the criticisms of the system cited by some include:

- It doesn't add anything to other loyalty related questions
- It makes use of a scale that has low predictive quality

- They feel it is not accurate, and that a composite index of questions might be a better solution
- It will not help to predict loyalty behaviors

Of course, you do not have to use this system of measuring loyalty alone. Instead, you might want to consider making it an overall part of your metrics along with other questions, for example. It could still be a good option to add to your company. As this book has hopefully shown you, the more information you have the better.

Listening Posts/Competitor Insight

What are people saying about you online? What do your customers think about your products or services? In the past, it would often be difficult to have a gauge of how your customers thought about what you offered unless they contacted you directly. You would not have been privy to conversations they might have had with friends, family, and peers.

Listening Posts

The digital age has changed this substantially. Today, when people have something to say about your business, good or bad, they post that information online. If you do not know the praises or the condemnations of your own company, it could mean trouble. Having listening posts through social media and with comments on your site and even review sites, provides you with near real-time information about customer reactions to your company.

The sooner you can thank someone who says they love your product, or help someone who has a problem or complaint the better. It will show that you are listening to their needs, and if there is a problem you want to make things right. This can help to build loyalty in a customer. Those customers are also likely willing to share good interactions they've had with your company, so they become an advocate for you.

Having listening posts set up for your brand can provide you with a range of benefits including the following:

- You can monitor your online brand image
- You can quickly and easily handle complaints
- You can find out what the customers want... and deliver on it.
- Keep track of trends
- You can learn more about what other companies are doing.

Competitor Insight

Learning more about what your competitors are doing can provide your company and your marketing department with some advantages. One of the worst things that a business can do, no matter whether they are brand new or they have been in their field for decades, is to ignore what the competition is up to.

You know that Coke and Pepsi are always watching one another. The same is true of any successful companies. They know there are some great benefits when it comes to watching the competitors.

Learn from the mistakes of the competition. See what they are doing right and wrong at all levels from products to pricing and marketing. Are they not meeting what their customers' need? This is where your company could come along and snag those consumers.

In addition, you can see what those companies are doing right. You can discover what works for them and then model your own company and marketing after them. This does not mean you want to copy what they are doing directly.

Take the good and make sure it works for your brand messaging. Use various strategies to help align most customers with your brand. Something else competitor insight will help you to glean is other opportunities in the marketplace.

Notes

By the end of this chapter, you should have a good understanding of both the buyer persona and the customer journey map. These are some of the most important elements in this chapter, as knowing your buyer's persona it can help you to gain more clarity regarding your ideal customers.

When you have a strong understanding of the customer's journey and the customer's thought process, it makes it far easier for you to create a great customer lifecycle experience.

CHAPTER 4

Problem

"People don't want to buy a quarter-inch drill. They
want a quarter-inch hole."

Theodore Levitt |
Former Harvard Business School marketing professor

The second P in the POINTS Method refers to Problems. Namely, these are the problems that your customers have and that your product or service aims to solve. You will find that Problems and People tend to be very closely related.

When you learn more about people, as we discussed in the previous chapter, part of what you need to understand is their problems and what they need. It is then the job of the marketing department to make sure that those people are informed of how your wonderful product can help them to deal with that issue.

In the digital age, most people head to the Internet to try to find solutions for their problems. You want their search to lead them right to you, and you want to be capable of truly solving the issue for them, as this increases the chance of them becoming a customer.

THERE ARE GENERALLY GOING TO BE FIVE STEPS WHEN IT COMES TO SOLVING A PROBLEM FOR CUSTOMERS

Identify the problem.. what market need are you trying to solve?

Analyze the problem

Look at the decision-making process of the persona

Provide multiple solutions

Refer the customer to the optimal solution

Where in the consumer journey is the problem located?

Image 15-Source ID: A15

How to Clearly Define the Problem to Solve

Of course, before you can solve any problems, you need to know what the customers need solved and how and why your product or service is the best solution. If you can't define and understand the problem, there is no way you can solve it, simple as that.

One of the best ways to understand what needs to be solved is by listening to the customers and researching your "ideal customer". What are they looking for? What do they truly need? What are their problems? Listen to what they say. How is your product or service able to meet their needs?

For example, if you were marketing for a gym, you would look at the type of services you offer – free weights, classes, personal training, etc. This is the base of what you can offer. You would then research customers to see what people want when they go to a gym. Keep in mind that different customers might have different needs and problems they need solved.

You will find that many of the people who are looking for a gym want to lose weight. Others might want to add muscle and strength. Some might want to do both. Others are trying to get healthy after their doctor recommended they come to the gym. Your job is to define the problems the various customers have by gaining insight through conversations online via email, social media, and the like.

Connecting with customers provides the human-to-human interaction we discussed. It also gives you information into how to reach customers with similar problems, even if they have not contacted you yet.

Once you clearly understand the problem, you can then let those customers know how you can solve those problems. Let's look at those who want to lose weight in the gym scenario, for example. You can explain how weight training in the gym is healthy for them and how it can change their body. You can talk about the various machines you have at the gym, and provide them with some nutritional advice.

Try to provide options for the customer, but steer them in the direction of the best or most optimal solution for their problem.

If you have a blog for your company, and you should, the blog can serve as part of the education and problem solving. A high value blog that helps to solve part of the problem through knowledge is fantastic. The blog lets the readers know more about your brand, and you are providing them with real value. This helps to encourage those potential customers to see you as a viable and trusted solution. You will find that this works for nearly any field or niche you might have.

SOME OF THE QUESTIONS
YOU CAN ASK
WHEN YOU ARE TRYING
TO DEFINE THE PROBLEM
THAT NEEDS
TO BE SOLVED INCLUDE

Where is the problem occurring?

What causes the problem?

When does it happen?

Who does the problem happen to?

Why is the problem happening?

Image 16-Source ID: A16

If you are having trouble defining the problem, take a step back and look at it from another angle or perspective. Ask the preceding questions, and you will find that you have a better idea of the type and scope of the problem and whether the products or services you offer can help.

Priorities and BIG IDEAS

In some cases, you might discover you are dealing with more than one problem that needs to be solved. When that happens, you need to prioritize which ones need to be addressed first. You should write down all the problems and then organize them by importance and urgency. Solve those that are the biggest or most important first.

If a customer has more than one problem, you will do the same thing. You will help them with their greatest problem first, and then help them with other problems.

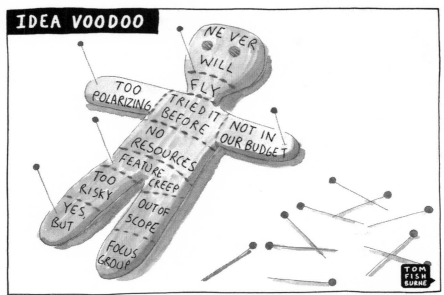

© marketoonist.com

Identifying the problem should lead your creative team towards ideation phases. Successful ideation should generate ideas to solve problems and tackle opportunities. This is why creativity is so valuable.

Notes

If you are following the POINTS Methodology correctly, by the end of this chapter, you should have determined the main problem that you need to solve, and then added a list of additional problems. Those additional problems should be put into a priority list, so you know which ones are the most important to take care of first. Has your team started ideating on possible ways to solve or tackle opportunities?

POINTS METHODOLOGY

All your efforts should be working toward a positive outcome. The best way to ensure you have success is by ensuring everyone on the team understands the situation they are trying to resolve.

CHAPTER 5

Purpose and Principles

"When you're surrounded by people who share a passionate commitment around a common purpose, anything is possible."

–Howard Schultz, Starbucks

What is the purpose of your company? It is important to keep in mind that the purpose of the company is not the company vision or mission statement. It is not even the company values. While there may be some similarities, it is important to understand the differences, as well.

A company's vision is a term often used to show what the company hopes to be or wishes to be in the years to come. The goal for a vision statement is to look years to the future and help to provide a way to think beyond the daily operations of a company.

A mission describes what the company is and now and in the future Importan. The goal of a mission statement is to provide focus for the staff and the management. Values is another term used quite often today. This will generally refer to the company culture and what those in the culture find to be important. Some have referred to values as a moral or behavioral compass for the company. Recently some human driven companies have embedded purpose in their clear vision statements.

The principles of the company help to provide the employees with the guidance they need to make sure the values are upheld and that the company stays on mission.

What about the purpose of the company? The purpose is what the company aims to do for their customers or clients. The following are some examples of company purpose statements.

- Google's mission/purpose is to organize the world's information and make it universally accessible and useful.
- The Wikimedia Foundation, Inc. is an international non-profit organization dedicated to encouraging the growth, development and distribution of free, multilingual content, and to providing the full content of these wiki-based projects to the public free of charge.
- Nourishing families so they can flourish and thrive. – Kellogg Food Company
- Empowering people to stay a step ahead in life and in business. – ING
- To help people manage risk and recover from the hardship of unexpected loss. – IAD

Here is a list that from HBR.org that shows some of the most important differences between a mission and a purpose. Think of the mission as "what we do", and the purpose as "why we do it". Your purpose is why your business has decided to make a difference, and it guides the actions the company takes.

Mission – What We Do

- Operating a Business
- Strategic
- Inspirational
- Creates buy-in
- Provides focus
- Building a company
- Laying bricks
- Parking cars

Purpose – Why We Do It

- Sharing a dream
- Cultural
- Aspirational
- Instills ownership
- Fuels passion
- Building a community
- Building "cathedrals"
- Creating happiness

Defining Your Company Purpose

Now that you have a better understanding of company purpose, it is time to start creating your own company purpose. You want the statement to define your company's core goals and what you can do for those who use your products and services. It should be succinct and easy to understand by anyone who reads it whether they are a part of the company or a customer.

When you are trying to come up with your purpose, you should ask a few questions. Why do you do what you do? Why does your organization exist? What is your company's cause? Answering these questions and then following the simple steps below can help you construct your company's purpose.

Here are some more steps that will help you to define your company purpose.

Think About the Customer

One of the primary things your company purpose needs to do is let customers know what it is you can do for them. Think about the customer's needs and who they are. What do they want and expect from the services you are offering? The purpose statement should reflect this.

By focusing on the needs of the customer, you are aligning Purpose with People. The statement should show how you can solve the Problem of a customer, too. However, you should not focus on a single problem for your purpose, as this will allow the purpose statement to be more flexible. You want to be able to meet the needs of the customer regardless of the products you currently offer.

Avoid Vague Statements

While you do not want to get overly detailed in the creation of your purpose statement, you also do not want it to be too vague. The purpose doesn't need to include every detail about the company, but the statement should explain what the company does and who can be helped by the company's services or product. Check out the included company purpose statements above if you haven't already.

Create Something Attainable

The purpose statement should not have goals that are unattainable and out of range, as it is impossible to tell if your company is making headway towards those lofty goals. The purpose statement should be possible and something that can be achieved relatively easily. Again, you can look at the construction of the purpose statements from the companies above to see how they are constructed and how we can see that those companies are in line with their purpose.

Core Strategic Values

The core values are what help to support the vision and the purpose of the company. They can help to shape the company culture, and are essentially the beliefs and principles you want the company to espouse. The core values can determine how the company is conducted internally, as well as how the business conducts itself in the outside world.

Often, you will find the core values are summarized in the mission statement, or in a separate core value statement.

The core strategic values of a company can prove to be important not only in providing direction for the company, but also in the way the company markets itself.

To get a better idea of what core values are, let's look at some examples from some of the most successful companies out there.

Zappos

- Deliver WOW through service
- Embrace and drive change
- Create fun and a little weirdness
- Be adventurous, creative, and open-minded
- Pursue growth and learning
- Build open and honest relationships with communication
- Build a positive team and family spirit
- Do more with less
- Be passionate and determined
- Be humble

Toms Shoes

- Give sustainably. Give responsibly.
- Giving partnerships
- Identify communities that need shoes
- Give shoes that fit
- Help our shoes have a bigger impact

- Give children shoes as they grow
- Welcome feedback and help us improve

Whole Foods

- Selling the highest quality natural and organic products available
- Satisfying and delighting our customers
- Supporting team member excellence and happiness
- Creating wealth through profits and growth
- Caring about our communities and our environment
- Creating ongoing win-win partnerships with our suppliers
- Promoting the health of our stakeholders through healthy eating education

Even though the core values of the company might be different, you can see their similarities and what the companies are trying to achieve. Look at these and other examples when you are coming up with core values for a company of your own, and be sure to think about the elements that are the most important to you, and that you feel might be important for the customers.

What Are Principles?

The principles of a company are the rules and/or values that help to guide the organization in determining what is right or wrong when it comes to their actions. Principles goes beyond the policies or the objective of a company. The principles are what help to guide the company in all of their dealings, internally and externally.

Make sure your team is fully aware and has adopted your companies values and principles. All ideas and initiatives will need to comply with your companies DNA.

Notes

By following the POINTS Methodology, you should have now mapped out the purpose of the company, or the project that you are developing. In addition, you should have a clear set of principles and values that will help to drive the company's day-to-day operations.

The clarity that you are developing provides your team with more focus. They know that their actions must be compatible with the organization's DNA.

CHAPTER 6

Partnerships

---

*"Our success has really been based on partnerships
from the very beginning."*

—Bill Gates

P artnership marketing has not received as much attention as other forms of marketing whether we're talking about branding, digital marketing, social marketing, or any other form of marketing. However, that does not mean you should ignore the possibility of partnerships. In fact, they could be quite beneficial to your organization.

What is a partnership when it comes to marketing? It simply means that more than one brand is collaborating in a marketing campaign to help one another achieve their goals. Often, there is a primary brand that has the best product or service to solve a problem, and a secondary brand that somehow complements the first. By working as partners, it helps both brands to improve their value proposition to the target audience.

A good example of two brands working together would be Mountain Dew and PlayStation. The marketing teams for these companies realized there is plenty of crossover between gamers and those who enjoy the highly caffeinated drink. Therefore, the marketing partnership they developed was very natural.

Quite often, you will see fast food franchises partnering with other companies, as well. Taco Bell has worked with Cheetos, and McDonald's has worked with Nabisco's Oreo cookies. You can find these sorts of partnerships in a wealth of places, and they are not always large, internationally known brands doing this. Look on the small scale as well. Perhaps a gym in your area is partnering with a local supplement store or a smoothie shop, for example.

Of course, there are many types of strategic partnerships that brands can use when working together, and we will be going over those in this chapter. Consider the current partnerships you have.

The first thing to do is look at any of the current partnerships your company might have with other companies and brands. These partnerships could be online only, or they could be part of your brick and mortar locations or both. Write down a list of all the partnerships you currently have. Are you using these partnerships effectively from a marketing standpoint?

In addition, list any potential types of partnerships you might want to develop and that you believe to be viable. Consider ways that you could create or expand your partnership that might be able to help the profitability and visibility of both companies. Remember, the partner needs to have a viable reason for working on the marketing campaign with you, and both of you must succeed and profit from it in some way.

© marketoonist.com

Map Out Your Current Partnerships

The steps for partnership mapping include:

- **Ecosystem Valuation** – Examines the impact of revenue with existing partner data.

- **Capacity Planning** – Determine the company and product growth expectations that could be fulfilled with partnerships.

- **Gap Analysis** – Determine what the partner might be able to bring to the table in terms of expertise or reach that your company can't.

- **Solution Mapping** – Determine the right resources to utilize when working with a partner and developing a marketing plan that can benefit both companies.

Partnership Marketing

When two entities decide to collaborate, they can help one another out in a range of ways. The following is a handy list of some of the ways that partners can help out each other's brands.

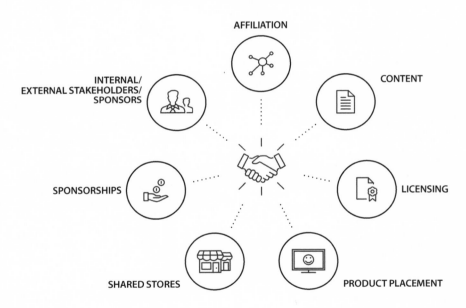

TYPES OF PARTNERSHIP MARKETING

Image 17-Source ID: A17

Affiliation

Affiliate marketing is a technique that is quite popular in the digital age. When you work with a partner, the partner will then promote your company on their website and/or their store. For the promotion, they will receive a portion of the sales made in most cases.

However, rather than paying the affiliate, some partners might reciprocate. They could promote the partner's products or services on their own site.

Affiliate marketing can take many forms including:

- Dedicated articles or posts
- Banner ads
- Text links
- Promo pages
- Newsletters
- Comparison tables

Content

Content marketing through a partner is possible, as well. Content is the lifeblood of the Internet, and your partner could host content on their site, such as blog posts or videos, about your products. Again, they could be paid for this type of service, or you could put their content up on your site.

In some cases, both brands might be behind the creation of the content. Other times, they may simply share links on the site. Some of the examples of content marketing with partners include:

- Articles
- Infographics

- Audio podcasts
- Videos
- White papers
- E-books

With online content, it is important for all the partners involved to understand SEO, so they can make the most of search engine optimization. This helps to ensure higher traffic to the page, and hopefully more attention for the brands.

Licensing

Another type of marketing can be done through licensing. This is often done with intellectual properties. For example, a cartoon might be approached by a company that makes toys, or a publishing company. The toy maker and the publishing company might want to license the rights to the intellectual property of the cartoon to use it in these other ventures.

Many different elements from a company can be licensed:

- Intellectual property, characters, etc.
- Logo
- Company culture

Product Placement

Product placement is another type of marketing, and this is one most often seen in the movies and on television. Soft drinks, fast food restaurants, auto manufacturers, and more have their products placed on screen for all to see. Product placement tends to be for larger companies that have the money available to pay their partners who will put them onscreen.

However, in some cases, the company with the product may offer the product free for that movie or television show in exchange for the placement. For example, they might provide the vehicles for the movie, or they may have their soft drink available free for those on set.

While these are traditionally used for Hollywood movies, the digital age has made it possible for people to create their own shows and movies online. It might be beneficial for some companies today to start reaching out to content creators online with product placement offers. Not all will be agreeable to this offer, but it should be possible to find some partners that have a large enough audience to warrant the cost.

The product placement could include:

- A logo in a scene or frame
- Direct mention in a scene
- Usage in a scene
- Background placement
- Placement in the foreground
- Endorsement by a celebrity partner

Shared Stores

Another option, albeit one that is not too common, is to share space in a single store. This occurs when a company has a store that offers space for another brand. This space could be rented by the partner, or it could simply be provided based on the agreement and what the partners do for one another.

This can occur online and offline alike.

A shared store might include:

- Promotional stands – This tends to be a relatively small stand for the partner. This could be permanent, or it could be a "pop-up" stand.
- Permanent desks – Banks in a grocery store, for example.
- Store in a store - Grocery stores that also have a Starbucks or a fast food restaurant inside of them.

When it comes to online stores that share space, offline shared stores are still more common than online shared stores. However, the concept of online shared stores is starting to grow.

Some examples of how this would work for an online store include:

- A member area – Featured brand partners could be placed in a member's only area that could also feature exclusive content and deals.
- Page or Tab – You could also have a dedicated page on your site for the partner brand, along with links to their site, if they have their own site.
- iFrames – Another option is to utilize iFraming, which lets you place the partner's website within your website.

It is likely that there will be new options and technologies that will help companies and brands to ally online and shared spaces. Keep abreast of the changes that come to this field and make the most of them when they are available to stay ahead of the game.

Sponsorships

The idea of sponsorships has been around for a long time. In fact, they were some of the earliest marketing techniques used, and they are still in use today – online and offline – because they can work so well.

A sponsorship can help you to raise awareness about a brand. It could also help to align a certain brand with a person, event, or a cause. Sponsorships can be large or small and they can be a part of many types of events or media.

The following is a partial list of some of the places where sponsorships can be found today.

- Sports
- Television
- Film
- Radio
- Podcasts
- YouTube and other videos
- Events (marathons, charity events, etc.)
- Local events and political rallies (this tends to be more helpful for smaller local brands)
- Websites (aligning with well-known and trusted websites as a place to stay, visit, or dine)

It can be a fantastic idea to think outside of the box when it comes to these, as you never know where a sponsorship might be able to help your brand grow.

One of the important things to remember about sponsorships is that you need to be transparent about the fact that it is a sponsorship whether you are the sponsor or the one who is receiving the sponsorship. Hiding the fact that you are being compensated is against the law.

Internal/External Stakeholders/Sponsors

In addition to learning how to work with partners, you must also understand who your internal stakeholders and sponsors are.

The internal stakeholders tend to be those who are on board with your organization and who are committed to the organization´s success.

Some of the prime examples of internal stakeholders include:

- Board members
- Employees
- Managers
- Investors
- Business owners

When running a company and developing a marketing strategy, it is essential that you understand who your actions in marketing, as well as the other actions of the company, can affect.

The objective of this exercise is to understand what talent you currently have available for your digital efforts and the type of executive sponsorship you are receiving from upper management.

Notes

By the end of this chapter, if you are properly following the POINTS Methodology, you should have a very clear understanding of your current partnerships. A detailed list of your current internal talent, stakeholders and sponsors is key to understand your gap analysis during the sustainment phase. This is essential because you want to truly know your current partner ecosystem. When you and your team understand the various partnerships and their roles, you will have a good starting line of options that can impact the marketing ecosystem.

We will be talking about partners further in the Sustainment Chapter, you may need to redesign the partner ecosystem for strategy fit.

CHAPTER 7

OKR – Objectives and Key Results

"The biggest impediment to a company's future

success is its past success."

Dan Schulman | *CEO of PayPal*

OKR, or objectives and key results, is the term used by organizations setting goals, as well as communicating and monitoring those goals. This is typically done on a quarterly basis. However, they can also be set monthly depending on the size of the company and its needs.

Who Created the OKR?

The OKR measurement was created by John Doerr for Intel. Many companies today utilize OKRs, and it is something you should certainly consider adopting.

What's the Difference with Objectives and Key Results?

An objective can be "qualitative or aspirational". They will generally take between one and three months to complete, which is why it is so common to have OKRs set up quarterly. The key results are qualitative. They can help you to get a better idea of how the objective was met.

When setting goals, it is important to choose those that are not overly easy, but are still attainable. There must be clear communication as to why you are setting the goal, and ideally, you will try to stretch the goal beyond what the company can usually do. This can help you to make additional gains over time.

In this chapter, we will be looking at the elements you need to consider when you are setting up these goals. It seems easy, and it can be, but there are many who rush through this phase and end up not getting the results they want for one reason or another.

In addition to setting up the goals, part of the OKR needs to make sure the company is connected and that everyone understands what is happening and what their responsibilities will be.

Most of the time, the OKR will have between three and five high-level objectives, and each of these will have three to five key measurable results listed. There is also a progress indicator for these objectives that ranges from 0% to 100%. The goal, of course, is to make sure that you have as high of a percentage as possible when completing the objectives.

If you do not like the idea of determining a percentage on your own, you can always choose a binary option instead. Use 0 and 1 in place of the percentage. 0 is for goals you are unable to attain, while the 1 is for those you do attain. Some find this to be less hassle. However, it might not give you enough information in all cases.

Now, let's look at ways that you can take further action to measure your objectives and results for your digital marketing. You will find that these methods can be used for other measurements in the company, as well.

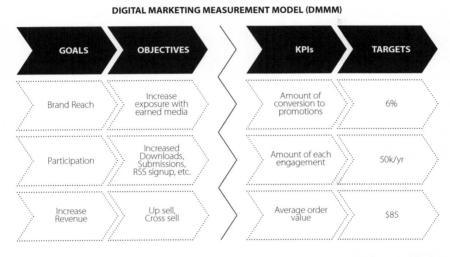

Image 18-Source ID: A18

SMART Methodology

SMART is an acronym that stands for specific, measurable, achievable, realistic, and time-based. This methodology has been a boon for companies of all sizes who utilize MBO, or management by objectives. It can help you with your marketing, digital and otherwise, as well. In fact, this type of goal setting has been utilized in a range of different fields because it works so well.

SMART GOALS GUIDE

SPECIFIC	What exactly needs to be accomplished? Why do we want to accomplish this goal?
MEASURABLE	How will we know we have succeeded? How much change needs to occur? How many actions or cycles will it take?
ATTAINABLE	Do we have the resources to achieve the goal? Is the goal a reasonable stretch? Is the goal likely to bring success?
RELEVANT	Is this a worthwhile goal? Will it be meaningful to management/the team? Can we commit to achieving this goal?
TIME-BOUND	What is the deadline for reaching the goal? When will we begin taking action?

Specific

When you are setting your goals, you always want to be as specific as you can be. The more specified you are, the better the chance of attaining that goal because you will have a better idea of what else you need to do to attain it.

To help you create specific goals, you and your marketing team should try to answer all the following questions, and any other questions that you develop.

- What do you want/need to achieve?
- How can you go about achieving it?
- When does it need to be achieved by?

- Are there conditions or limitations?

- Who is working toward this goal and what are their jobs?

Measurable

Measurable goals, which we will talk about in detail later in the chapter, simply mean you can track what's happening with your efforts to determine whether you are making any headway. If the goal you set is not measurable, it is virtually impossible to determine how you are doing. There should never be a question as to whether or not the goal was attained.

Achievable

Of course, you need the goals to be something that you can attain. The goal of becoming the biggest company on the planet or outselling the Big Mac in your first year of business is not only lofty; it is extraordinarily difficult to reach.

Do not have goals that are impossible to reach! The goals you have should not be extremely easy to attain, but it should not be out of the realm of possibility either. If you set the goals too high and make them too difficult to reach, you will never reach them. You and your team will become discouraged, and this can seriously hamper your efforts. When you have a team that suffers from low morale because they are never able to achieve their goals, their productivity and creativity are very likely to suffer.

Realistic

This aligns with having achievable goals. These are goals that are challenging, but those that you can still reach. They should be able to be accomplished by the time, tools, and personnel who are working on the objective. If they aren't, you are choosing an unrealistic goal. You need to change it. Again, goals that are unattainable are going to cause frustration.

Time-Based

Rather than saying you want to improve your sales turnaround by 15%, you want to be more focused when you are setting your goals. You want to give yourself a time limit. Say you want to increase by 15% over the course of the following year, and then measure the goals to see where you are each quarter. When you set goals that have a time limit attached to them, you will find that people often strive to meet and beat this goal.

Later in the book, we discuss gamification and how it can help with the marketing processes. However, you will find that it can also be quite beneficial when it comes to setting goals for your team. Having goals that they can reach, milestones they can achieve, and perhaps rewards for doing extremely well, can go a long way into making them happy.

Measurable Goals

Regardless of what you might want to achieve, whether it is improving your results with your digital marketing efforts, or even losing weight, you need to make sure you are setting measurable goals. As we discussed, this is one of the key elements of the SMART methodology.

If you are uncertain about how you are doing and progressing, you may never know when you have accomplished your task. You will not know whether you are off the rails and having problems, or if you are close to achieving your goal.

What do you need to do to measure the type of goal you want to attain? Understanding how you will measure the goal is essential. Understand the quantity you are after and whether there is a standard you need to reach to achieve the goal. How clear can you make the goal? When the goal is clear, you will find that it is often easier to measure your progress.

Benefits of Setting Measurable Goals

When you have measurable goals you are working toward, it can provide you with some nice benefits.

First, it can increase the motivation you and the others on your team feel. When you can see that you are making progress toward your goals, it makes people want to work even harder. They see that they are closer to achieving success. In addition, it can provide a small amount of pressure, which can help people to produce results.

Another one of the benefits of setting goals that you can measure is that you can spot weaknesses and problems. If you find that you are not making any progress, it means something is not going according to plan. You can then make the needed changes sooner rather than later, which can help to keep you going in the right direction.

Having measurable goals and working toward them with your team can also help to create stronger teams. Everyone is working together to reach the results they need, and they are helping one another to do so. This includes not only the marketing team, but everyone else in the company who wants the product or service to succeed. While it is a collaborative effort regardless of the goal measurements, the measurements do help to keep everyone on track.

Challenging Goals

When someone is setting goals, whether it is for his or her team or themselves, there is the temptation to make the goals a bit on the easier side. People want to make sure they can achieve their goals, so they set the bar low. However, this is a huge problem whether it is for your marketing team or in your personal life.

Setting a goal that is not a challenge is a goal that is probably not worth doing. Why should you settle for mediocrity when you could be striving for greatness? You want to make sure the goals that you choose can challenge your team and make you work hard. You will feel better when you achieve those goals, and your company will be the better for it.

However, you do not want to commit the reverse problem and make the goals so challenging that you will never be able to achieve them. You need to set a middle ground. It needs to be something that can be accomplished, but it can't be a simple task the even an entry level marketer could achieve. Always challenge yourself, and you will get better and more confident.

Check out some of the best athletes in the world to see how that works. If Michael Jordan or Peyton Manning set easy goals, they would not be remembered. Always strive to do the (almost) impossible.

Market Potential

One of the most important objectives of marketing is understanding the marketing potential, or MP, of a product or service you are working to sell. The market potential will give you an idea of how much money can be made from that product or service in the locations where it is being offered.

Of course, the market potential is an estimate, and that estimate can only be as good as the information used to develop it.

- Define the target market
- Define the geographic boundaries
- Define the competition
- Define the market size
- Estimate the market share
- Determine average annual use/consumption
- Estimate the average selling price

Now, let's take a closer look at each of the things needed to figure out what the market potential will be.

Define the Target Market , go back to your Buyer Persona

By the time a marketing team is ready to determine the market potential, they should have already defined the target market for the product or service. Knowing your target market is an essential step that anyone in business today needs to follow.

To find the ideal customer target, you can look at the current customer base to see what common characteristics clients and customers share. In addition, you should look at what your competition is doing. Who are the competitors targeting and who are the current customers? You do not have to go after the same customers. In some cases, you will be able to find a niche that will work better for you and that competitors are overlooking. We have previously discussed buyer personas, make sure your team has mapped out they key characteristics of those who are most likely to make the purchase.

Some of the demographics elements you need to consider include:

- Age
- Location
- Gender
- Level of income
- Level of education
- Married/single
- Type of job
- Background

The psychographics are important to understand when you are trying to target the right audience for your products, as well. Psychographic elements include:

- Attitude
- Behavior
- Interests
- Lifestyle
- Personality
- Values

When you have a better understanding of the psychographic make up of your audience, it is easier to know how your service or product would fit into their life. By understanding the psychographics, you can have a better idea of the type of media they use when they are searching for information, how and when they will use the product, and what features they like/want the most.

All these elements are helpful to the marketing team, as they can provide more of a direct connection with the consumers.

You want to do a good job of breaking the target down to get an understanding of how well a product can do, but you do not want to break the target down into a niche that is too small and that would not justify the marketing effort.

Define the Geographic Boundaries

Where will you be selling the product? Are you only selling or providing a service in the local area, or do you offer shipping across the country and around the world? Understanding your geographic boundaries, including not only the location, but the population density and demographics mentions earlier, can help you when creating a marketing plan.

Some of the factors to consider when defining your geographic boundaries include:

- Neighborhoods based on U.S. Census block data
- City boundaries
- County boundaries
- National boundaries
- State borders
- Zip codes

For example, if you have a small company that offers an offline service, such as running a local gym or spa, your geographic area is often limited to your town and nearby areas. You would likely want to spend a lot of your marketing efforts on getting locals to come into your establishment.

However, if the down you happen to live in is Aspen or Miami, or another hot tourist spot, you can also expand your geographic market to target people outside of the geographic area, but who will be traveling to your town.

Understanding your geographic reach can help you to determine how much money you could make based on the product or service you offer. Keep in mind that a service that is used multiple times, such as the gym membership we mentioned, can keep on providing profit. In fact, the longer a person stays a member of a gym the cheaper it was to acquire them as a customer.

However, goods or services that are used rarely or only once are going to generate less profit as the number of remaining customers shrinks, which we will discuss further in the section on defining the market size.

When you have a well-defined, local geographic area, such as those who have only or mainly brick and mortar establishments, you will find that local SEO, which we discuss later, can be very important.

Define the Competition

Your competition are all the other companies that are selling the same types of products or services that your company does. You are often striving to get the same clients and customers, all with the goal of increasing revenue and growing your business and your brand.

The market competition helps to motivate companies to increase their sales, often by somehow altering one of the four Ps:

- Product
- Place
- Promotion
- Price

For example, you could add a new product, or service as the case might be. You could change the price, do a promotion, or offer the services or products in another place. All these would help you to deal with the competition. Of course, the competition is going to be doing the same, so dealing with the competition is truly a never-ending battle.

You must know who all your competitors are and what they offer their customers. Know their strengths and their weaknesses and learn from them. There are several types of competitors.

- Direct competitors
- Indirect competitors
- Replacement competitors

A direct competitor would be someone who offers the same products and services that you offer to the same market. An indirect competitor may products or services that are not the same, but that could satisfy the same customer need. The indirect competitors also tend to have a different means of driving the revenue. A replacement competitor offers a different product or service, but one that could still replace yours.

Take the time to know who your competitors are and what they can offer to customers and clients.

Define the Market Size

The market size is the number of people in the market who are potential buyers for a product or service. You naturally want to know the market size of an area before launching a product or a marketing campaign in a particular geographic location.

When you are determining your market size, you need to realize that not all people who are in your area will become buyers or clients. Not all people will want or have need of the types of services you can offer. Therefore, the work you did with demographics can help you to get a better idea of your true market size.

In addition to defining the market, you also need to determine which approach you feel will work better to determine your market size.

- Top-down
- Bottom-up

The top-down market approach utilizes a broad market size figure and determines the percentage represented by the target market. The bottom-up approach totals the variables in the target market to build the total available market, or TAM. While this second method takes more time to complete, most feel that it is a better and more accurate option than the top-down method.

Estimate the Market Share

When you are estimating the market share, or the market potential, it lets you know whether your company can support their business and cover all their costs. The market potential is the number of potential buyers, an average selling price, and how much of the product or service the buyer will use in a given amount of time.

There is a basic formula that can be used to help you find the market share. This formula is used by many different types of companies.

$$MP = N \times MS \times P \times Q$$

In this equation:

- MP = Market Potential
- N = Total Number of Potential Customers

- MS = Market Share (Percentage of Customers Buying from Your Company)
- P = Average Selling Price
- Q = Average Annual Consumption

When you use this equation, you should have a better understanding of what your true market potential will be. This does not mean you won't be able to break expectations, but you do want to have a realistic idea of what you should expect.

Determine Average Annual Use/Consumption

The average annual use or consumption is going to vary greatly based on the type of product or service you are offering. You will need to have a firm understanding of your offerings and how your consumers tend to use the products or services. Just look at how much these could vary from one type of product/service to another.

- Food is consumed regularly, and a customer might continue to buy throughout the year on a weekly or monthly basis.
- A gym membership can be paid monthly or annually in most cases.
- An electronic device, whether it is a phone or a fan, is generally bought once every couple of years.
- A book is typically bought just once

As you can see, the annual use can be drastically different based on the type of items you are marketing for your company. You may even have several items from one company that would fall into different consumption categories. Make sure you differentiate between them.

Estimate the Average Selling Price

The ASP, or average selling price is the price at which a good or service is usually sold for. The type of product, and the product life cycle can affect the average selling price, naturally. Therefore, items such as computers, cameras, and jewelry will typically have a higher price than books, Blu-ray disks, and most types of food. The four stages of the product life cycle include:

- Introduction
- Growth
- Maturity
- Decline

Supply and demand can also affect the selling price, as well. Supply and demand should not affect the average selling price, though, as companies should always strive to meet the demands of their customers in the primary market.

Market Potential and Objectives

When you look at the market potential for the goods and services that your company is selling, it should provide you with a range of objectives that you and your team can strive to reach. Keep in mind all the factors that figure into the MP, and then make sure you have achievable objectives you are trying to reach, as was discussed earlier in the book.

Historic Method

Another way to work on your OKR is to look at the historical data from your company, and even from competitors. This tends to work well when you have a large amount of historic data from which you can glean information.

If there are competitors in the field, you might only be able to find surface data from your observations, but it can still be helpful. Another term used when working with historic data is forecasting.

You can see the growth of the product, and then look at ways that you could have improved upon the marketing of that product or service. You can also start to pinpoint potential future trends, which can help you when you are trying to determine the OKRs for your product and marketing campaign.

Of course, this is not a method that will work well for all companies, as those newer companies will simply not have enough historic data of their own, and they may not have enough from the competitors for that matter.

The FTE (Full-Time Equivalent) Method

FTE is a method used to measure how many full-time employees it takes to perform work done at a company. Not all companies hire only full-time employees, even for the marketing department. Therefore, you need to know how you can determine the number of equivalent full-time employees so you can better utilize those resources.

Full-time employment is 40 hours of work per week. To get the total number of FTE workers, you will calculate the number of hours worked per period by the full-time workers, and add that to the number of hours worked by the part-time employees. You can then divide the total by 40, which will provide you with the number of FTEs you have available.

When you know how many of these workers are available, you can then delegate more easily, and you can create objectives that can be accomplished by your team, so you can get the results needed and reach your goals. It ensures that you are neither underutilizing or overworking the team.

Reevaluate Your OKRs Before Committing

As you can see, you have quite a few things to consider when you are developing your OKRs that you want to achieve. Fortunately, the digital age has made is not only easier for you to reach the people you are marketing to, but also to gather all the information you need when it comes to developing your OKRs.

Consider the information and advice in this chapter regarding the different methods that you can use, and find the one that works the best for your company and the types of products you are trying to market.

Remember, there is no single best way that is going to work for all companies when it comes to developing and reaching their key objectives.

© marketoonist.com

Notes

Those who are correctly following the POINTS Methodology should now have mapped out your goals, objectives, and the key result utilizing the SMART Methodology. In addition, you should have matched those goals, objectives, and key results to each stage in the customer journey – Awareness, Consideration, Purchase/ Action, Retention, and Advocacy.

As you are aware of by this point, it is about far more than just understanding the problem. It is about creating detailed context of the objectives along each stage of the buyer's journey to provide you with the best results. Creative ideation has to be aligned with business interests. Your ideas and actions must generate business results.

CHAPTER 8

Initiatives

"In today's era of volatility, there is no other way but to re-invent. The only sustainable advantage you can have over others is agility, that's it. Because nothing else is sustainable, everything else you create, somebody else will replicate."
— *Jeff Bezos, Amazon founder*

© marketoonist.com

Before the ad tech and digital phase, marketing/ advertising model mainly revolved around four Ps (4P Model). However, many theories have developed, collapsing the older models, after the tech boom in recent years and from these some highly effective models have been derived. Here we are going to discuss two rather successful and important models namely PESO and INBOUND.

POINTS METHODOLOGY / DIGITAL MARKETING BLUE PRINT

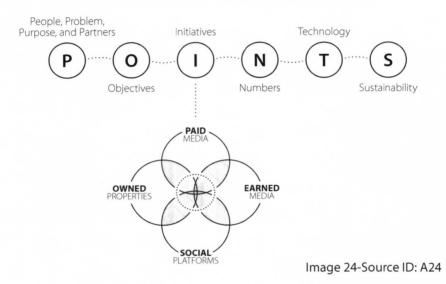

Image 24-Source ID: A24

PESO Model of Marketing

This is a relatively new model, although it has been somehow in the use since 2008, it was not presented officially until 2014 when digital marketing expert Gini Dietrich published her book Spin Sucks and proposed the PESO model in it. Since then this model has been very well received and has been a success for many business and marketing firms who have used it.

PESO is a highly effective method because in its complete understanding it is basically an acronym for a big-picture and all-channels-inclusive method of communication and this is the only way in which any business, company or entrepreneur can reach all the stakeholders that have relative importance. PESO stands for Paid, Earned, Shared and Owned media. Just the complete form of this acronym in enough to tell us its importance, however, it also shows the vast level of marketing channels that this model covers. By implementing this model any business can jointly utilize all four major channels of marketing and PR and it will be able to monitor its collective effectiveness at a larger and wider scale. PESO model is considered to be a jack of all marketing channels and with the right execution, it can very easily be turned into the master of all marketing channels too.

Let's break down what these individual channels quickly:

INTEGRATED MARKETING ECOSYSTEM

Image 25-Source ID: A25

Paid: It is any media platform/channel to which money or resources are paid for distribution and marketing.

Earned: Earned refers to the publishing of content or coverage of any business or enterprise by a credible third party such as a newspaper, media channel, blogger etc.

Social (also called SHARED MEDIA) : This channel is a platform for sharing and passing along of information regarding any business/venture using social media.

Owned: This is the personal source of any business or company through which they generate their content and then advertise it, such as a company's own website, blog, content writers etc.

By understanding these four mediums of marketing it gets quite clear what benefits this model has to offer. One of the most important benefits that PESO model allows any marketing team is an authority. It gives authority to the team over their complete marketing network, all four main channels and their subsidiaries where the team can monitor, evaluate and increase the productivity of their marketing model and along with this, they can control its gains as well, using calculated algorithms. This position of authority is not easily achieved otherwise in businesses, especially in the fields of marketing and sales.

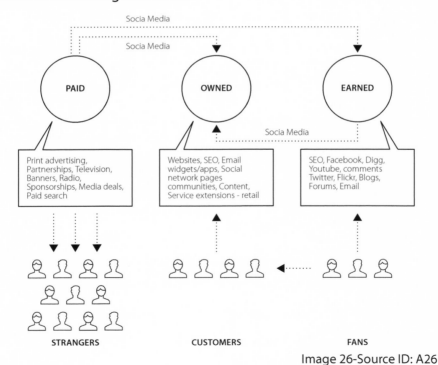

Image 26-Source ID: A26

In addition to the authority, this model works with a dual-benefit power mechanism. This is possible in such a way that out of the four basic channels of marketing, the two (shared social and paid) channels work on the principle of 'Power of multiple mediums/individuals', which means that they use different websites, blogs, journals, and many other mediums to project a certain brand or execute a marketing plan, this gives the marketing team a chance to utilize this power in the best possible way. The two other channels (earned and owned), work on the principle of 'On individual's power' where the content of a single valuable individual can create a vast beneficial difference in the marketing gains.

Utilized to its potential, PESO model collectively benefits the marketing efforts of any business, product or entrepreneur.

Implementing PESO model to its complete potential is not as easy as it sounds. It requires a strategic execution. Starting with market research, planning, and hypothetical execution to the incorporation of all four media channels into one giant media strategy, this model requires extensive brainstorming by marketers and PR officers using market and customer knowledge and then testing it with the PESO model hypothesis.

Different industries use different examples and practices to implement this model in accordance with their product's demand and customer knowledge. There are certain techniques very commonly used by marketers for the PESO model.

Brain Storming

Any planning phase generally starts with brainstorming ideas, sharing these and then hypothetically applying these to the model and calculate the results. Marketing firms usually start their planning by brainstorming ideas. These ideas are then employed in a theoretical plan where these are tested for their effectiveness. A tricky yet very easy thing about brainstorming is that any idea is acceptable as long as it co-related with the complete process.

For every media channel in the peso model, different ideas are brought forth and then co-related with their counterparts to visualize the results.

Organizing the Ideas

After the brainstorming phase for the PESO model, all the selected ideas for every media channel are then applied to a completely hypothetical working PESO model. The key for these ideas to be incorporated into the final plan is for them to be co-related to each other, in line with their brand personas and target audience finally these ideas are supposed to work in such a manner that these ultimately interconnect the four main media marketing channels into one elaborate plan. Companies usually use different tools for this process such as a procedural chart or whiteboard with an elaborate flow chart for the complete process.

Tracking the Progress

After the hypothetical PESO model plan comes out to be successful, it is then employed into the market as a working PESO model. The only thing that is required now is to track the progress of this model. For this process companies usually divide the four channels to different teams who then track the progress of every channel and then integrate this progress into the overall success of the PESO model.

When a marketing firm starts working with the PESO model, it comes up with an elaborate plan on how to conquer and make the best use of all these four media channels. It takes into account different strategies of fully using these channels for market domination of their product or brand.

Paid Media

This is any form of media for which a brand has to pay for its utilization. Some examples of paid media include paid search results, paid advertisements, and sponsorships. Although this content is created by the brand it is promoted by channels, which aren't owned by it.

Benefits

Paid media targets the customers, which are not necessarily searching for the brand but might be interested in the services and products it has to offer. Also what content is displayed by paid media to customers is controlled by the brand.

Examples

Paid Advertisements

These adverts can virtually appear anywhere. These adverts may be in the form of a full banner or even a small link. Brands can also pay for ads to be displayed during broadcasts, videos or on pages of other companies.

Sponsorships

This typically entails some kind of financial or incentivized support by a brand in return for its public acknowledgment through different means.

Best Practices:

a) Be creative

b) Intelligent use of social media

c) Be precise and to the point

Earned Media

Earned media is perhaps one of the most viable forms of media available to any brand. As customers are more likely to trust promotion by any party that is not directly related to or owned by the brand. Earned media includes word of mouth, unsolicited reviews and trending content.

Benefits

Due to the reason that earned media is not owned by the brand itself, it has more impact on customers and they are more likely to be convinced by it. Also if and when used properly it has the potential to reach and influence more customers than any other media channel.

Examples

Un-Solicited Reviews

These reviews of a brand usually appear on a customer's own website or any third party website, blog or social media page. These reviews are very powerful and are capable of influencing opinions than any other brand.

Viral Content

Viral content usually means that it is being shared by people across the globe it can be in the form of an article, images, videos or blogs.

Best Practices:

a) Respond to feedbacks appropriately

b) Create content users want to share

c) Promote word of mouth through loyal customers

Social Media, also called Shared Media.

Social media is similar to earned media but it is more efficient in generating quick marketing results. It generally comprises of creating a positive image of yourself through your content in social media interactions, the only difference is that social media is much faster and has more reach than earned media. Social media included social media channels such as Twitter, Facebook, blogs, Instagram etc.

Benefits

Shared media reaches customers faster than any other form or media, therefore it has more impact and it influences a wider market of customers. Also shared media somewhat entails the use of almost all the other three form of media channels.

Examples

Twitter

Twitter is a fast and wide-ranging social media platform reaching to ordinary people and trendsetters (people of influence) all at the same time. Any viral trend on twitter is sure to bring in customers.

Facebook

Facebook is one of the most famous and adverts friendly social media platform, millions of people use it worldwide. Marketing teams can gain immensely positive results from proper utilization of Facebook.

Best Practices:

a) Create attractive content

b) Choose the appropriate user market

c) Use loyal customers on Facebook for furthering brand marketing

Owned Media

All those channels, websites or blogs owned by the brand itself are part of owned media. These include company website, blogs or social media profiles.

Benefits

The most important benefit is that the brand itself controls and maintains this form of media. Brand decides the content to be posted and how to interact with the user.

Examples

Websites

Brands use their websites to offer customers services and knowledge about their product. Along with this, these can get customers to sign up for promotions and incentives as well.

Social Media Profiles

This platform allows the brand to connect with their customer on a more personal level and it encourages consumer engagement through two-way communication.

Best Practices:

a) Interact with customers

b) Connect all channels to one another

c) Offer useful and interesting information

All the four media channels of the PESO model have their individual contributions to any marketing firm's overall marketing strategy. Putting it very simply these four media channels are the four basic pathways and pillars of media marketing world. They encompass every possible and important media sub-platform, which is required to reach any type of audience across the globe. Once a firm strategizes through defining their buyer persona that what type of customer market they want to target, after that it will make use of these four platforms to connect with that specific brand of customers. These four media channels allow marketers to utilize it in any way they deem suitable for the sole purpose of designing their marketing strategy around the functioning of these media channels.

After a marketing firm identifies its customer brand, it will analyze the means through which each of these media channels will be able to affect those customers. Then they will measure the effectiveness of these channels with their desired results and after thorough calculations, it will then utilize the 'Power of One – Power of Many'

(Owned and Earned – Paid and Shared) theory, which was explained above in this chapter. Marketers will pour sufficient resources into the power they feel will be able to bring them more positive results and they will utilize that power into their final marketing strategy.

Marketing firms set different criteria to measure the success of marketing campaigns of all four platforms. We are going to explain some of these the impact of any marketing campaign and its results.

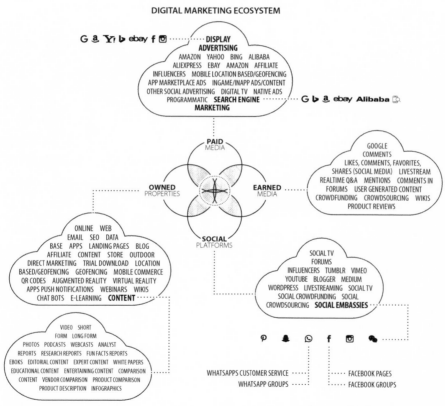

Image 27-Source ID: A27

Customer Satisfaction

Customer satisfaction is the main goal of any marketing campaign because only by achieving this goal will a product be able to attract and increase its user base. Customer satisfaction can be measured by different brand surveys, customer feedback, and general product demand or by asking customers fragmented questions the answers of which will determine customer satisfaction.

The Response of Customers

Customers are of utmost importance to any brand or company. A company measures its success and gains its sales and profits through these. Therefore customer satisfaction and an increase in the user market is the final aim of any marketing plan or model. Thankfully different theories have identified the basic journey a customer takes when it interacts with any brand. This journey contains the following steps.

a) Awareness

b) Discovery and Consideration

c) Purchase or Action

d) Retention

e) Advocacy

Now one of the most important parts of any marketing plan is to observe and evaluate this journey and create ways to ensure that a customer's journey through your brand is pleasant. In order to do that, certain touch points are identified and developed through which this journey is observed and evaluated. These touch points relate to different stages of the customer journey.

POINTS METHODOLOGY

Stages and Touch Points

Awareness and Discover Stage

Touchpoints:

a) Reviews (Social/Shared Media)

b) Social media interactions (Social/Shared Media)

c) Word of Mouth (Social/Shared Media)

d) Testimonials (Social/Shared Media)

e) Marketing / PR (Social/Shared Media) (Paid Media)

f) Advertisements (Paid Media)

Purchase Stage

Touchpoints:

a) Store / website / office (Owned Media)

b) Current promotions (Paid Media)

c) Point of sale (Owned Media)

d) Catalogue / brochure (Owned Media) (Paid Media)

e) Staff/sales team interaction (Owned Media)

Use of Product and Bonding Stage

TouchPoints:

a) Marketing Emails (Owned Media)

b) Online help desk (Owned Media)

c) Invoice (Owned Media)

d) Service/support team (Owned Media)

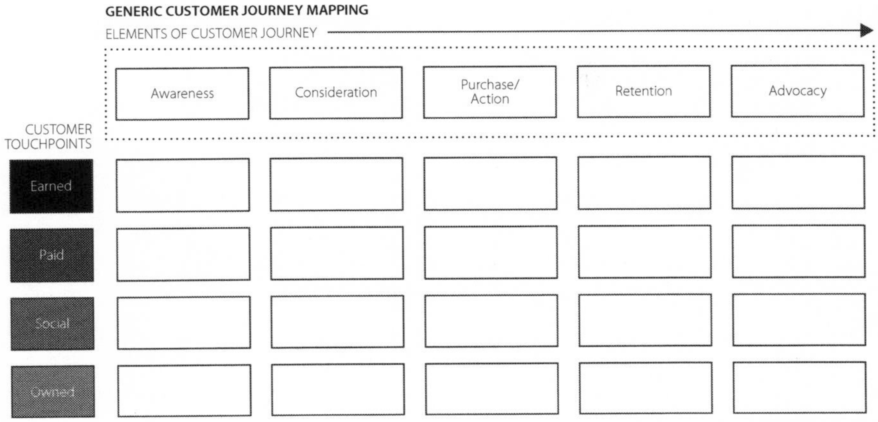

GENERIC CUSTOMER JOURNEY MAPPING

ELEMENTS OF CUSTOMER JOURNEY ⟶

	Awareness	Consideration	Purchase/Action	Retention	Advocacy

CUSTOMER TOUCHPOINTS

Earned

Paid

Social

Owned

Image 28-Source ID: A28

All these touch points are monitored manually and digitally in terms of customer interactions, customer response, customer awareness, visits of the customer on pages and websites, Customer visits to stores, follow-ups of customers on links, advertisements, articles, incentives, and promotions. All this is monitored digitally as well as physically to determine more effective results and ensure customer satisfaction.

As the PESO model is a combination of four main media marketing channels therefore in order for this model to work all these channels have to work in synchronization with each other. Without their synchronization this model will not be able to generate positive results, rather it will be difficult to even implement it properly. The reason is that in one way or the other these four channels are inter-connected moreover, majority of the customer base of any product uses almost all of these channels for different purposes, therefore if any one channel is not in synchronization with its counterparts then that will negatively affect the customer, their opinion and as well as the marketing plan.

Many companies sometimes focus on either one or two media channels to target their customers due to which their customer attraction and generation is relatively low than other companies in the market. Imagine if a customer is deciding to choose from two brands of the same market, one brand utilizes all four media channels to attract the customer through intelligent and positive advertisements/marketing whereas the other brand utilizes only two or three of these channels. The difference of impact on the customer will definitely be greater and more positive regarding the first brand leaving the second brand at a loss.

Other than this if these four media channels are not interconnected with each other, the PESO model will not be utilized to its full potential and desired results will not be achieved. PESO model is a very effective model. Its utility has been proved numerous times in the marketing world. That is why it is being used by marketing firms all around the world. It is certainly a very innovative and beneficial induction into the world or Media Marketing.

Buyer Persona and Inbound Model

In order to get efficient results from the inbound model, a different yet unique approach is used sometimes where the marketing team after studying the user thoroughly through different surveys

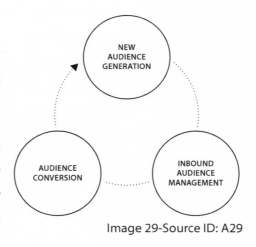

Image 29-Source ID: A29

and processes develops a 'Buyer Persona' through which they understand their user and implement that understanding in the model.

As already discussed in the third chapter, a buyer persona is a fictional or semi-fictional character, which is based and developed on the knowledge gained from market research and real-time data regarding a product's existing users. While creating a buyer persona, you need to know the user behavior, demographics, goals, motivation, preferences, and literacy rate, and demand patterns. A buyer persona gives a detailed insight into the company regarding the user based on which a detailed marketing plan can be developed and implemented. This will help the company in aligning their target audience through which they will be able to attract the most valuable users and loyal customers.

The inbound marketing model implementation is based on this persona; therefore, it will strongly determine the user experience at different stages.

Buyer personas help marketers in yielding successful results once these are used with different marketing techniques. Buyer personas assist marketers in different phases/procedures of their marketing plans. One of the very basic yet quite successful marketing technique is 'Inbound Marketing'. Marketers are very well aware that inbound marketing yields successful results if you are able to successfully implement its four pillars.

Inbound Marketing Basics

As discussed above in this chapter, inbound marketing is one of the most essential forms of marketing nowadays. This is so because inbound marketing teaches us to directly target the most important resource for any company/business that is their 'Customers'. Inbound marketing works with four basic principles.

Attract:

Good businessmen and marketers are well aware of the importance of customers and their satisfaction, as because of these customers their brand even exists in the market. Therefore, this stage is all about understanding your buyer market and attracting the right type of customer. Customers want to feel acknowledged, they want to interact with the brand, learn new things and make deeper connections and only those companies survive in the long run who provide their customers with what they wish for. In order to successfully interact with these strangers, companies normally use what is known as buyer personas. With the help of buyer personas the ideal buyer is outlined and then marketers start to concentrate upon this specific type of buyer, they use their content through different types of media channels to attract these buyers to their product. Consider the type of content your buyers will likely prefer during different stages of their buyer's journey i.e. awareness, consideration and decision stage. This phenomenon is known as 'Buyer Persona Content Marketing'.

Different media channels you can use to attract visitors:

1) Social Media

2) Blogs

3) Websites

4) Keywords / SEO

Techniques you can use on these channels:

1) Develop emotional connections

2) Build a community or forum

3) Use technology to your benefit

Convert:

After the successful implementation of the attraction phase, your buyer will be directed towards your site, blog or social media page, this is where you need understand that simply attracting customers/ audience is not enough for good marketing and sales, you need to be able to convert these leads into customers. You will require their personal information, this is the tricky part because normally people do not give out their personal information and in order to get it, the company will need to provide them with some valuable information or content that will appeal to their taste so that in return they will be willing to give you their personal information. The content you share with them can be in the form of guides. E-books, articles etc. So that they can start trusting your brand.

Some useful methods/techniques to convert visitors into leads are:

1) Call to Action (CTA)

2) Contact Database

3) Landing Pages

4) Expand your marketing channels

5) Know your target audience

6) Stay active and interactive

7) Develop interesting/appealing content

Close:

So by now, your hard work has paid off and you've successfully converted visitors into leads. Here comes the time to close these leads, which means turning them into customers, here you need to determine that whether or not your leads are capable of becoming valuable customers, will they be able to represent your brand positively and how strong would be their word of mouth. This is the stage where nurturing your leads gets you the most results. You can take help from the buyer personas that were previously made and with that information you can provide your leads with useful content and information at the right time. In this phase, you will at first have to nurture the customer and address their needs; in short, you will have to boost the customer egos. This will be a stepping stone in lead closing.

Some important ways and market channels for closing the leads are:

1) Be empathetic and real towards your audience

2) Use automation tools

3) Make customers part of your team

4) Lead Scoring

5) Email Marketing

6) Customer Relationship Management (CRM)

Delight:

After you've successfully made your sale all you need to do is to show a little more determination because this determination will take you miles ahead of your competition who after making their final sales are relaxing now if you take this final step then your gains will be unmatched.

What you need to do here is to turn back again to your valuable customers and start interacting with them. Try to make a connection with them, show them that you care about their experience with your product, you care about their opinion and their suggestions and you care that they make an affiliation with your product. This is how you'll get them to stay and come back for more, this is also how you'll get them to become your brand ambassadors and their word of mouth will benefit your company more than you can think of. All you need to do is to delight your customers not just physically but emotionally as well.

Some useful ways to achieve this are as follows:

1) Email Marketing
2) Social Media Marketing
3) Feedback / Surveys
4) Questionnaires
5) Brand Events
6) Offers, Promotions, Test, Brand Activities
7) Make empathy and kindness a part of your team
8) Make customers a part of the team
9) Value their opinions/suggestions

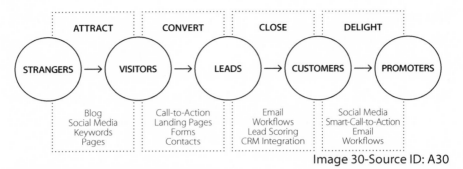

Image 30-Source ID: A30

Content is Always the King

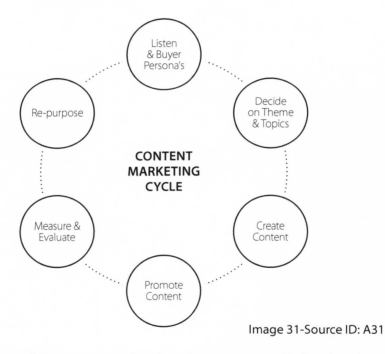

Image 31-Source ID: A31

Take a note of this quotation by Shai Aharony CEO of Reboot Online, he says: "Content is the backbone of any drive to interact with your readers or customers. It is the most important opportunity you have to impress the reader with your knowledge, expertise or ethos. The quicker the publishers realize this, the quicker their websites take the place they expect in the industry of their choice." This saying clearly identifies the importance of content in today's world of media/content marketing.

May this content be in the form of articles, blogs, images or even videos but content stands second to none when it comes to its importance in today's marketing world. Whatever you write or post on the internet regarding your product or business, it falls into the category of content and that content is viewed by millions of people around the world, now whether they see/read it and what they do after that is totally dependent upon the quality of that content.

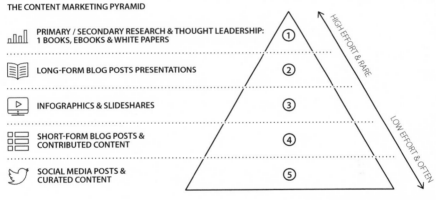

THE CONTENT MARKETING PYRAMID

1 — PRIMARY / SECONDARY RESEARCH & THOUGHT LEADERSHIP: BOOKS, EBOOKS & WHITE PAPERS

2 — LONG-FORM BLOG POSTS PRESENTATIONS

3 — INFOGRAPHICS & SLIDESHARES

4 — SHORT-FORM BLOG POSTS & CONTRIBUTED CONTENT

5 — SOCIAL MEDIA POSTS & CURATED CONTENT

HIGH EFFORT & RARE

LOW EFFORT & OFTEN

Image 32-Source ID: A32

A company or brand should focus on developing high-quality content and that too regularly. This is so because the content is the first thing any customer will see or read when they will start looking for your brand and this interaction will determine whether this consumer will go on to become a loyal customer or will they just scroll down with disappointment. There are many ways to prevent this from happening, for starters, content development should be of high quality, easily accessible and it should be appealing to customers. In order to develop high-quality appealing content, the company can use knowledge gained from buyer personas to realize the type of content that would be in line with the preferences of their user market. Other than this there are a few main reasons why content is important in today's marketing business:

Enhances SEO

When high-quality content is produced, it is viewed more and shared more. Google starts giving more opportunities to bring up your page or blog in front of best results.

Enhances Engagement

Whether it is blogs, websites or social media pages good content will always encourage users to interact more with the brand. They will gain a sense of belonging and feel a part of your brand if you will interact with them through genuine content.

Generates New Leads

New customers are always confused and have a lot of questions. Good quality content works in two ways over here, at first it attracts these customers towards the product and once they start following the product it starts interacting with them answering their questions and clearing their doubts, in this way the customers feel welcomed and valued. This, in turn, increases their customer satisfaction and starts generating new leads.

Increases you Value

A satisfied customer is a loyal customer and a loyal customer is a good brand ambassador. This will increase the value of your product in the social circle of your users and your brand will start getting more leads as well.

Increased Traffic

The last stop of this cyclic process is a massive increase in online traffic. Good content will ultimately start bringing in more visitors to your blogs, websites and social media pages. This increase in traffic will increase your brand value, bring in more customers and ultimately it will increase the sale of your product enhancing your user market.

Check out this content creation and amplification worksheet as a guideline to create repeatable content pieces:

CONTENT INITIATIVES WORKSHEET

PERSONA (choose 1)	
YOUR TOPIC/KEYWORD (choose 1)	

CUSTOMER JOURNEY PHASE (choose 1)

Awareness ☐   Inform ☐   Commit ☐   Loyalty ☐   Advocacy ☐

HOW WILL THIS HELP YOUR BUYER PERSONA?

FORMAT/TYPE (choose 1)

eBook/Whitepaper ☐   Template ☐   Checklist ☐   Comparison Chart ☐   Case Study ☐   Worksheet/Calculator ☐   Podcast ☐   Video/Webinar ☐   Purchasing Guide* ☐

CONTENT STRUCTURE (choose ≥ 1)

List ☐   How-to ☐   FAQ ☐   Best of ☐   News/Trends ☐   Q&A ☐   Opinion ☐   Curated ☐   Product-focused* ☐

CONTENT TITLE

DISTRIBUTION

AMPLIFICATION BUDGET

Image 33-Source ID: A33

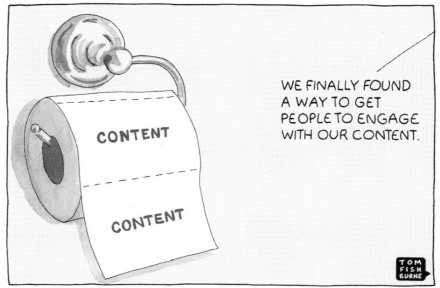

© marketoonist.com

Notes:

In this chapter, we discussed two basic marketing models the PESO and INBOUND models. These two models are totally dependent upon two basic but very important pillars 'Customer' and 'Content' and surprisingly these are the two most important pillars of the principle of marketing. Both these models demonstrated the importance of customer satisfaction through content making use of different media channels. PESO model was focused on utilizing the different media channels to promote your brand to customers and turn them into loyal users with the help of content. It was a very successful model and it is still used worldwide by numerous businesses. The INBOUND model focused solely on customer satisfaction / nurturing and how we can reach it by managing and converting the new inbound audience into our loyal customers by the end of their buyer journey.

By the end of this chapter you should have a clear idea of your tactical initiatives.

The following quick checklist will help you with your initiative fundamentals:

- Are you able to locate each initiative in the PESO model?
- Are you able to locate each initiative in the customer journey stages?
- Do you have a clear understanding on how each initiative will help your organization achieve the previously set goals and objectives?
- Do your initiatives match your values?
- Do you have too many initiatives? Focus on the 80/20.

CHAPTER 9

Numbers

---

*"We must realize—and act on the realization—that if
we try to focus on everything, we focus on nothing."*
–John Doerr, Measure What Matters

Many find numbers to be less exciting than content or making videos. In fact, most people likely think that way. However, the numbers are extremely important if you want the POINTS Methodology to work for you. The numbers will give you a better idea of how you are doing with your content and your marketing plan, and they can let you know if you need to make any changes to get back on the right track.

Failure to pay attention to and learn from the numbers often translates to failure in your marketing campaign and ultimately in your company. In this chapter, we will be examining the most important facts and numbers you need to consider when you are trying to improve your company's success and reach.

KPIs

KPI, or key performance indicators, are measurable values that show the effectiveness of a company when it comes to reaching key business objectives. Many companies utilize KPI´S as a means to see how successful they are when it comes to reaching certain targets, but it will depend on choosing the right KPI for your initiatives.

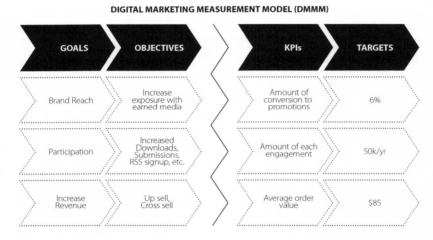

DIGITAL MARKETING MEASUREMENT MODEL (DMMM)

GOALS	OBJECTIVES	KPIs	TARGETS
Brand Reach	Increase exposure with earned media	Amount of conversion to promotions	6%
Participation	Increased Downloads, Submissions, RSS signup, etc.	Amount of each engagement	50k/yr
Increase Revenue	Up sell, Cross sell	Average order value	$85

Image 18-Source ID: A18

Types of KPIs to Track in Marketing

There is a saying that the only way you can improve something is by measuring it. This simply means that you need to know where you stand in order to see if you are making improvements. In marketing, there are plenty of key performance indicators you will want to follow and track. Some of the most important include:

- **Sales Growth** – Of course, this is one of the top KPIs that any company wants to measure. Are you getting more sales now than you did during the last quarter? If not, what happened and what can you do about it?

- **Leads** – You want to have new leads constantly coming into your company, and you want those leads to become customers eventually. Keep track of this KPI, as well.

- **Lifetime Value of a Customer (LTV)** – KPIs can help you to get a better idea of the lifetime value of a customer, so you know how much their business is worth. You can calculate this with a simple formula – Revenue x gross margin x average # of repeat purchases.

- **Cost of Customer Acquisition (COCA)** – How much are you spending to acquire each of your customers? The goal of this is to keep lowering the amount that you are spending for each customer, naturally.

- **Response Time of Sales** – How long does it take sales to get back to customers? This is a performance indicator you want to keep as low as possible. Customers tend to be happier when the sales team has a fast response.

- **Leads from Website** – You have a website or blog, and you hope that it is providing you with traffic that becomes leads. A great KPI to have is tracking the number of leads you have that come from website visitors. From there, you will want to see how many of those leads become customers.

- **Website Traffic** – Ideally, you will have a constant increase to the number of visitors to your site or blog. Tracking this information can provide you with insight on when you need to improve your content.

- **Social Media** – Just how well are you doing on social media? Are you gaining more followers, and are those followers actually buying products or services from you?
- **Email Performance** – Check to see how people are responding to the emails you have sent out.
- **Blog Post Visits** – How many people have visited your posts in the past, and how many are coming to read your posts now? The goal is to have an increasing number of readers to your blog each time you take measurements.

All of these are very important when it comes to a company's success, so make sure they are a part of the KPIs you are measuring. Analytics tools can help you with your measurements.

Find the metrics that are important to your company and start measuring them. Always strive to make improvements, and understand that it will take time and work to make those improvements happen.

© marketoonist.com

Scoreboards

Another way marketers are measuring their effectiveness with the various marketing channels they are using is through the use of scorecards or scoreboards. These cards make it possible to monitor, report, and improve performance on various channels and metrics that you need to track. Keeping track to make improvements is one of the areas where most marketers feel inadequate and as if they are not doing a good job.

When you are building your scoreboard to measure your effectiveness in marketing, you need to do several things.

First, you have to find the most important KPIs for your business. What are the five most important KPIs to you? They should be connected to your business goals and your marketing should be trying to achieve those goals.

Once you have your list, you will want to input and analyze your data from sources such as your marketing or CRM software, Google analytics, social media analytics, and email marketing information.

When you see how you are doing, you will then set your benchmarks and create a list of the most important goals to reach. Then, you simply monitor your progress and update the scoreboard to see how you are doing. Hopefully, it will always be going in a positive direction for you, but that might not be the case.

If you notice your scoreboard is not in your favor in certain areas, do not fret. It is an indicator that you need to make some changes to get things back in order. The scorecard can be a powerful tool, so make sure you use it as such. You can create template cards for each of the areas you need to measure.

Small Data and Big Data

With the arrival of the digital age, the terms small data and big data have become part of the common vernacular. It is important to understand what each of these means, and what each of these means when it comes to marketing. First, we will start with small data and then work our way up to big data.

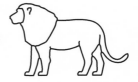

SMALL DATA

Low Volumes,
Batch Velocities,
Structured Varieties

BIG DATA

Into Petabyte Volumes,
Real-time Velocities,
Multistructured Varieties

Small Data

Small data, as a term, came after big data. It is essentially slices or pieces of big data that are manageable enough to be actionable. Small data is also small enough that it can be comprehended which means it tends to be easier to act on.

It relies on data acquisition and data mining so you can then create smaller sets of data. These tend to be far easier to wield for a person or a team than big data is, simply because of the scope.

The use of small data is commonplace for the healthcare field, as well as for marketing endeavors. The specific data sets used can provide marketers with focused information on their target audience. This information can then be used to market specifically to certain people or a group of people. As you can imagine, the information you receive from small data is a powerful addition to any marketing campaign.

According to Martin Lindstrom, who wrote the book Small Data, this type of data "has the power to trigger emotions and to provide insights into the reasons behind behaviors of customers." It has the potential to help reveal the "type" of person, such as whether they are extroverted or introverted. As you can imagine, this sort of information can be highly useful for marketing.

When focusing on small data, you will find that it can allow predictive insights to become more practical, which means you can act on them with better results. In Lindstrom's book, he also defines the 7Cs. He believes that companies should use these to help them gain more meaningful insights, as well as market trends.

The 7Cs, according to Lindstrom, are:

- **Collecting** – The information that is collected needs to be understood on a customer-level basis rather than a group basis to learn more about who the customer is and what they do.

- **Clues** – Look for more information that can provide a deeper emotional insight into the client.

- **Connecting** – Learn to identify the consequences of emotional behavior.

- **Causation** – What is it that causes the emotions to occur in the customer in the first place?

- **Correlation** – When was it that certain behaviors and emotions were noticed in the subject?

- **Compensation** – Once you have the data, it allows you to have a better understanding of the customer's problem and what they want. You can create marketing the promises to fulfill that need.

- **Concept** – The concept is the act of defining what the customer needs.

When used properly, small data can be a huge benefit for companies of all sizes. It is easily available, and it is easy to decipher and understand. This means you do not have to have someone with an advanced degree just to parse all the data and make it useful. You are not working with vague ideas, speculation, or hypotheses. You are working with known facts.

Some of the types of small data collected from customers include:

- Addresses
- Phone numbers
- Contact preferences
- Personal information

Small data does require analysis, but it is far more manageable, and it is possible to use it with various marketing tools that you might already have in place.

The small data tends to be more accurate and up to date than the big data, as well. As you are likely aware, incorrect data can cost a company a substantial amount of money. Even if just a small percentage of your data is inaccurate, it is wasted time and money on the part of your marketing. The accuracy of small data helps to reduce waste.

This type of data is essentially "ready to go" for marketing, which means you can implement it quickly and easily. While you can certainly see how utilizing small data can be useful to a business, especially for the marketing department, big data has some benefits, as well.

Let's examine some of the other reasons businesses like to utilize small data:

- **It's easy** – When compared with big data, taking and using small data tends to be easier and faster.

- **Small data and human to human work well together** – We work to build our relationship with the customer today, and small data is certainly a big part of that. It also combines well with CRM and the tools that we utilize to help with that.

- **ROI** – Small data tends to have a great ROI – it's easier to obtain, and it can provide you with some fast, positive results in many cases.

- **Tools** – More tools are becoming available for this type of data, which will eventually make it even easier to use.

Data is essential for your business now, and it is going to continue growing. In today's world, you can't get away with not using data driven marketing, so it makes sense to embrace small data now and reap the rewards it can offer.

Of course, we can't forget the benefits that big data can offer, as well.

Big Data

Many people feel that big data is one of the most important and influential trends for businesses in the past decade. Most of the experts also agree that big data is only going to get bigger in the coming years.

Big data is a collection of data from both traditional and digital sources from outside and inside the company. The amount of data in the world today is massive given the types of technologies we use and the sheer number of people in the world who are contributing to this data simply by going about their normal lives.

Many feel big data is just about digital data. While that is where the bulk of the focus lies, you will still want to remember certain types of traditional data, such as paper transaction information or financial records.

Types of Data

Big data could be **unstructured**, or it could be **structured** and **multi-structured**. Unstructured data is information that is not organized, and that tends to be more difficult for a traditional database to interpret. Some of the most common types of unstructured data gathered today tend to be tweets on Twitter, as well as other social media posts, and metadata. Multi-structured data could include weblog data, which includes text and images, forms, and other channels of interaction.

Big data might take longer to understand and to parse than small data, but it can be quite helpful. It can help companies to make better and faster decisions in many departments, including the marketing department. Big data can be collected from many sources including:

- Servers

- Databases
- Applications
- Mobile devices
- Social media
- Sales
- Website interactions
- Emails

Once the data is captured, it can be formatted, analyzed, and used by marketing and other departments in the company. Proper utilization of big data can improve operations in a company, but it does take more of an investment than working with just small data.

It is often easier to work with an analyst, or a team of analysts, when using big data. Software tools can make it easier to analyze the data, but it can still be a challenge given the volume of data and the different formats collected across the organization. The first challenge is to break down the data silos (data in a single department). The organization also needs to have platforms and methods for gathering unstructured data just as they gather the structured data.

Benefits of Big Data in Your Business

When you are using big data, you can find actionable insights. These insights will provide you with information that can be used by various departments, including marketing. This data can then help you to do the following:

- Increase the company efficiency

- Boost sales
- Improve customer service
- Improve marketing
- Help to manage risks.

You can be sure that other companies are starting to utilize big data, including your competitors. You do not want to fall behind, and if you neglect all this informative data, that's exactly what will happen.

Which Is Better for Marketing – Big or Small Data?

While there is a massive difference between small data and big data, both can be useful for marketers. Big data has the massive size and volume. It provides you with the ability to gather unfathomable reams of data to use, while small data provides you with key insights that you can use.

You can think of big data as an army and small data as a special operations unit – both can help to get the job done. Rather than choosing one over the other, you should instead find ways that you can embrace both big and small data and bring them into your company's marketing plans.

Analytics and Predictive Analytics

Analytics in marketing includes technology and processes that can help the marketing team determine how successful they are with their marketing efforts. Analytics can measure performance of the various marketing outlets used by the team, such a social media, blogging, and the like. Analytics makes use of many important metrics, such as the ROI, or return on investment, marketing attribution, and overall marketing effectiveness.

Analytics can take data from all of the marketing channels and consolidate it so you can see it in one place. This information is like gold for the marketing team because they can see where they are being effective and where they need to make some changes and improvements.

Today, this information can be gathered quickly – in a matter of seconds in many cases. This gives marketers real-time information that they can use to make changes faster and easier than ever before. It takes away the guesswork, which is financially sound and very efficient.

Marketing analytics will allow you to see how your marketing efforts have performed over time, today, and into the future. You can get a better idea of how you compare with the competition. You can also research to see what channels the competitors might be using that you have not tackled yet.

The analytics can help you figure out what you need to do next. You can make sure your marketing resources are allocated properly, and that you are putting effort into continuing with and improving the marketing channels that are doing well for you.

You want to report on the past, analyze the present, and predict the future. That is where predictive analytics will come into play.

What Is Predictive Analytics?

Predictive analytics is the technique of using data and stats to determine the potential future of certain outcomes based on historical data. The goal behind this type of analytics is to get an idea of what is going to happen down the road if you continue on your current path or make certain marketing changes.

While it seems a bit like Nostradamus trying to predict the future, there is actual science behind the field. This method of analytics has been around for many years, but it has improved and become more accurate in the last decade thanks to things such as faster computers, better quality software, and better data. Today, companies can utilize analytics software and have a good idea of what the future can bring.

Predictive analytics has been utilized to help with a range of different problems that are often difficult to solve. It has helped to detect fraud, improve operations, reduce risk, and improve marketing campaigns. The predictions can determine what a customer response will be and whether they will make a purchase, all based on past data. With this information, it becomes possible to attract the right types of customers and to grow their loyalty.

Keeping Data Safe

You want to make sure your data is safe and easily accessible, whether it is small data or big data. Having data loss or a data breach can cause massive problems for any company. Your customers and clients will no longer trust you with their information, for starters. It can greatly hamper your ability to do business.

It is important that you take steps to safeguard the data your company holds long before anything happens.

First, you need to make sure your data is recoverable, and that you can access it around the clock, no matter what happens. Cloud backup and tape backup can both be helpful. The more safeguards you have in place for recovery the better.

Working with remote data centers can also help to disaster-proof your data. Fires, earthquakes, floods, and other issues have the potential to wipe out data. Ensuring you have duplicate data offsite, as well, ensures that even in the event of a disaster at your place of business, the information is safe and work will be able to continue.

Ideally, you will never be without access to your data, even in the event of a problem, for more than 24 to 48 hours. Any longer than this, and it can have a significant impact on your business.

Make sure the companies you choose to help you with your data storage, backups, and recovery truly have the means to safeguard your information, and that they are within your budget. Keep in mind that in cases such as this, the budget should really be a secondary factor. Safety of data is always the primary concern here.

When you are choosing a company for your backups, it is important to make sure they are secure and compliant. Make sure they encrypt your data, which can keep it safe even if someone unauthorized were to get their hands on it.

Having onsite and offsite backup is essential in today's world. If you do not have quality backup and tools for your data, it could come back to haunt you. Having trusted ways to keep your data safe is well worth the cost.

Notes

At the end of this chapter, if you are following the POINTS Methodology, you should have assigned KPIs to each element in the perfect combination of paid, owned, earned, and social.

Tracking is essential, and it should be an established discipline in your company. By continuing to pay attention to and incorporate analytics, it should help you to become more predictive and proactive, while being far less reactive.

By now you must have figured you need great technology to keep pace of your customer journey and your initiatives effectiveness.

CHAPTER 10

Technology

"At least 40% of all businesses will die in the next 10 years... if they don't figure out how to change their entire company to accommodate new technologies."

— John Chambers, Executive Chairman, Cisco System

We've now come to the "T" in the POINTS system. The technology that you choose to use when marketing and gathering information has the potential to make a range of tasks substantially easier. Not using technology, or using the wrong technology, can do the exact opposite.

When you factor in big data, as well as the various marketing channels available, there is massive potential for marketers of all stripes. Of course, when it comes to technology, there are always certain challenges that need to be overcome before they can provide a true benefit.

Challenges of Integrating Technology

In this chapter, we will be discussing a range of different technologies that could help your business including the cloud, various platforms for different tasks, and much more.

One of the first challenges is explaining to the decision makers at the company why certain technologies are essential. They often worry about another challenge – the cost of the technology – and it can sometimes feel like an uphill battle trying to get them to understand and agree that new tech can help the company's bottom line.

Yet another challenge is getting the employees at the company to learn the technology and to add it to their workflow. Many people, especially those who are set in their ways, are averse to change and to additions of technology they do not know. It can sometimes be difficult to get them on board.

You need to explain to those employees, as well as the decision makers for that matter, how much the technology can benefit your company and why it is so essential.

In addition, when you introduce any technology, even if you might feel it is simple and intuitive to understand and learn, you must provide training for everyone who will be using it. This will cut down on confusion and mistakes.

In addition to the effect of technology on people at your company, consider how it will affect your customers and prospective customers, as well. Your customers know that marketing is integrated in to just about everything they do, especially on the web. Regardless of the tech and platforms you use, it is essential to remain transparent about your marketing.

You will also want to understand that consumers eventually become "ad blind" and they start to ignore some types of marketing. That's why it is important to keep up with technology and to find new and better ways to truly connect with and reach those customers.

Marketing Automation Platforms

With all the factors and tasks encompassed in marketing today, it is very helpful if you have some type of marketing automation software that can help you with the multitude of responsibilities you need to handle regularly. There are many options available today, so you will need to find the one that you feel is right for your marketing needs.

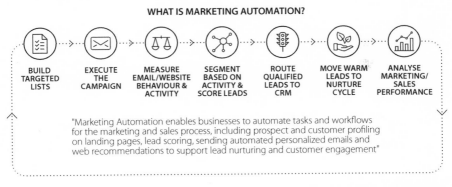

WHAT IS MARKETING AUTOMATION?

BUILD TARGETED LISTS → EXECUTE THE CAMPAIGN → MEASURE EMAIL/WEBSITE BEHAVIOUR & ACTIVITY → SEGMENT BASED ON ACTIVITY & SCORE LEADS → ROUTE QUALIFIED LEADS TO CRM → MOVE WARM LEADS TO NURTURE CYCLE → ANALYSE MARKETING/SALES PERFORMANCE

"Marketing Automation enables businesses to automate tasks and workflows for the marketing and sales process, including prospect and customer profiling on landing pages, lead scoring, sending automated personalized emails and web recommendations to support lead nurturing and customer engagement"

Image 19-Source ID: A19

Tips for Choosing the Right Marketing Platform

Let's look at how you can narrow your choices and find the option that will work the best for you.

First, you want to make sure you have a plan in place and that you know exactly what you need before you even start to look at the platform options. It's common for marketers to want to rush when choosing a platform so they can get started with it, but that is a big mistake. What ends up happening is they buy into a platform that is not capable of handling all the tasks they need.

Before you choose a tool that you think will solve a problem, understand and write down everything you are trying to solve. Consider everything you need to do in your marketing campaigns, whether it is creating blog posts, posting to social media, improving relationships with the customers, etc.

Know what you need and what your marketing plan will entail, so you can compare it to what the marketing platform will have to include to be viable for you. Ideally, the automation tool can serve more than just the marketing department. You may be able to find software platforms that can work for marketing, as well as for sales and customer service. Having everyone working on the same platform helps to keep everyone in the company on the same page. Finally, you want to make sure you have a platform that is relatively simple to use. If it ends up being too complex, people are not going to want to use it. Try to keep it to the essentials and perhaps some of the areas where you are planning to expand.

Software can provide a range of options. Some of the features you might need to have with your automation software include:

- Lead nurturing
- CRM integration

- Segmentation
- Forms
- Landing pages
- Marketing lead database
- Social listening
- Automated email response
- Email personalization
- Online behavior tracking
- Customization

Of course, your needs could vary from these substantially. As mentioned, you will want to find something that works well for you and has the features you need.

Marketing Platform Options

Many platforms are currently available for marketing automation. With all the choices, it can be difficult to find the ones that have the best options. We've provided a list of some of the top platforms currently available. Keep in mind that these are just some of the options out there, and you may want to continue your research and find other choices that better reflect your needs.

Marketing Automation Myths

While marketing automation is growing in popularity, so are many of the myths surrounding this tool. It is important to understand and to dispel these myths so you have a true version of what to expect.

Myth #1: You Only Have to Do It Once

This is a myth that can get marketing teams into trouble. Even though it can make things easier for you, it is essential that you maintain the automation process and keep it running. The automation process doesn't mean that the computer is going to churn out your posts and your updates. You still need to put in a substantial amount of work if you hope to reach your goals. Consider it to be a supplement for your marketing plans, not a way to get out of work.

Myth #2: It Only Works for Email

Another myth is that people believe it is only useful for email. Those people who believe this have not really done their research to see all of the other avenues and channels where this automation can help.

Myth #3: It Lacks a Personal Touch

Some fear that using this type of marketing makes it feel impersonal and cold, and they worry that their customers will not respond. If that's the case, it is because the marketing team did not do a good job setting up the automation.

In fact, when you automate, it should be easier to be more personable to your clients in newsletters and emails, as you can segment your audience and even address them by name in your communications. Imagine how much time this would take if you were to attempt to do it all manually! You can be personal and get it done faster with automated marketing.

Myth #4: People See It as Spam

Some might believe the myth that automated marketing is nothing but spam. It's true that spam is a problem, but proper automated marketing is certainly not spam. The marketing communications set up with the methods in this book are requested by the customer. They come looking for your company. They sign up and agree to emails and newsletters, as well as other communications, so it is not spam. They want to receive these messages.

Myth #5: It Is Not Worth the Cost

Companies are always trying to find ways that they can reduce the amount of money they are spending, and they might feel that automating is not necessary. After all, can't the marketing team handle everything?

You have to explain that the cost of the software is miniscule compared to the benefits it can provide. Explain these benefits, and how much more efficient the marketing department can become. Most will quickly see that a good piece of software for marketing automation is well worth the cost.

Use It the Right Way

How Can Marketing Automation Help You?

When you use it properly, marketing automation can be a very powerful tool in your arsenal. Whether you are using it for a small business or a large business, it has some impressive benefits that can make it possible to run complex marketing campaigns that are targeting a range of different types of customers. Since you will not have to take care of this manually, it truly does help to simplify things.

The following are some of the biggest benefits you can enjoy when you choose to automate at least some of your marketing:

- **Save time** – When you choose to use automation, it is possible to create several campaigns, as well as posts for blogs and social media ahead of time. You can schedule them for the future so you are not always running against the clock. Of course, whenever there is breaking news in your field, you can add those posts manually.

- **Customize communication** – Another one of the great benefits to marketing automation is that it is easy to reach each of your customers through automatic segmentation, lists, custom emails, and more.

- **Your staff can do more** – When your staff is not trying to do everything manually, they will have more time to take care of other marketing matters. Since the staff can take care of more with greater efficiency, it also means you are saving money.

- **Easier to be consistent** – One of the issues that many companies have when it comes to digital marketing is being consistent. They miss posts for social media and the neglect their blog for a few weeks. These things can kill the momentum of a business. When you are able to automate and have these things written and ready to go in advance, it is far easier to remain consistent.

- **Detailed reports** – Perhaps one of the biggest benefits of marketing automation is that it can provide you with reports about each of the campaigns you are running. You can see how every aspect of the campaign is doing at a glance with stats, data, and often graphs.

- **Consistent branding** – When you are working on multiple channels, it can sometimes be difficult to keep the branding message and look the same for all of them. When you automate your marketing, it is much easier to keep things consisted in your campaigns across the channels.

- **Improve relationship with the leads** – You can nurture your leads when you automate your marketing, just as you could manually. However, you can connect digitally, which makes it much faster, and since your leads are online anyway, they are more accustomed to this type of communication.

- **Build customer profiles** – It is possible to generate stronger customer profiles, since this type of marketing can make gathering customer data simpler. This leads to better segmentation and the knowledge you glean can help to improve your future campaigns.

- **It's Easy** – You will also find that the software for automating your marketing tends to be quite simple and straightforward. You should not have much trouble getting started and coming to grips with the software.

CRM

CRM is the acronym for customer relationship management, and you had better believe that it is vital in the digital world, just as it is in the brick and mortar world. In fact, some might even argue that it is more important now that everyone is on the Internet because problems with the customer can quickly be exacerbated in ways that were not possible before the web.

CRM systems are pieces of software that can help make working with customers, no matter how large your company might be, easier and more personable. They will allow businesses to better manage their relationships with customers, as well as the information and data associated with those customers.

What Can CRM Software Do?

Quality CRM software will allow users to store information about their customers, as well as about prospects. They can create accounts for the customers, and the software can also allow them to have lead and sale information all in a single package. Many of the options are available in the cloud, which means you can access it from anywhere with an Internet connection. The following is a list of some of the many applications that are often included with CRM:

- Customer data
- Customer interaction information
- Automated sales information
- Lead tracking
- Contracts

- Marketing
- Customer support
- Client and contact information
- Vendor and supplier information
- Employee information
- Knowledge and training information
- Other resources and assets

These are some of the features often available when it comes to CRM software. You should consider what your company needs when you are looking for a piece of software that can help.

As you can see, this type of software is highly valuable, and it can make many aspects of running a business smoother and easier. It can help businesses of all sizes, even those you might think are currently too small to benefit.

If you do have a small business, choose a simple CRM that does just what you need, and make sure it will integrate into the other company systems.

What Should You Look for With CRM Software?

When it comes time to choose a CRM system, there are certain guidelines you will want to follow to make sure you are choosing one that is right for your company.

- Ease of use
- Integration
- Remote/Mobile access

- Security and recovery
- Analytics
- Customization
- Scalability

Ease of Use

One of the top things you should consider when you are choosing a CRM system is the ease of use. You want to have a system that is as simple to use and to integrate into your company as possible. If the system happens to be hard to use and overly complex, you can be sure your employees will not want to use it, thus rendering it entirely ineffective.

It is possible to create some in-house training programs for the software, and you should, but if the system is too complex, you will end up wasting too many resources and too much time for the training. Search for something simple, and see if there is a trial or demo that you can check out. This will give you a better idea of how it will truly perform.

Integration

You must also think about the integration. Even if you have a simple CRM tool, if it does not integrate with the other systems already in place, it will not do your company much good at all. You should check to see that it will work with the marketing software you are already using, along with any other pieces of software or applications that might be used at the company.

If there are conflicts, you will likely want to look for a different CRM, as it is easier to find a single new piece of software than replacing everything you already have set up and running.

Remote/Mobile Access

One of the great things about the digital age is the fact that you can work from just about anywhere… so long as the software allows for it. This is where the cloud comes into play. When you choose a CRM in the cloud, you can access the information you need no matter where you might be. You just need to have a connection to the Internet to use the software.

This can be a nice solution for those who tend to travel quite a bit for their job, and those who need to do some last-minute work while they are at home or on the road. Without remote access, it will be difficult to get the data you need when you are sitting in a client's office or at a convention or tradeshow.

While there are certainly some fine CRM offerings that do not allow for mobile and remote access, they could be something of an inconvenience for you.

Security and Recovery

When you start to use a CRM, you are collecting information and important data about customers, clients, and other associates. This information is often private, and you would not want it to fall into the wrong hands. Your customers feel the same way.

For this reason, you need to make sure the CRM you choose offers security. It needs to have the capability to protect the data from an array of cyber-attacks, and to prevent loss of data. In the event of data loss or an attack, the CRM should offer data recovery. You can never be too careful.

Analytics

In the next chapter, we will be delving into analytics. For now, know that the CRM you choose to use should provide you with the ability to check analytics and to run reports. This is how you can get a better understanding of everything that is happening in the company and with your customers. This can help you to make smarter, informed decisions.

A good CRM will allow you to generate reports from the analytics quickly and easily, and they will have a range of reports that you can create.

Customization

Your company and your needs are going to be different from all the others out there. This means that there is not likely a single CRM that can meet all your needs right out of the box. Therefore, you want to choose a CRM tool that allows you to customize the software here and there so that it works well for your company.

CRMs should allow things such as changes to the dashboard, as well as the contact field and lists. Some have levels of customization based on the tier you choose, and others may have premium templates that you can use and alter to fit your company's needs.

Scalability

You should always be looking to the future with your company. Your needs today may be different a year or two from now, and you want to be sure you have a CRM tool that can scale with those needs. Find a tool that can grow alongside your business, and that is capable of meeting your needs as you reach different goals in the future.

When you have a scalable CRM, you will not have to worry about changing it out and choosing a new tool in a few years when your company outgrows it. If you don't, you will have to go through the entire process of finding another CRM before you know it.

However, just because you choose one tool now does not mean you can't change in the future if you want to. Perhaps a new piece of software will come out in a couple of years that will work better for your company and it meets all of your requirements. In those situations, make the change that's best for the company.

Great Options for CRM Software

Now that you have a better understanding of the types of things you should be searching for when buying a CRM tool, it's time to start your research so you can narrow down your choices. The following are some of the top options today when it comes to CRM.

- HubSpot CRM
- OnContact
- Salesforce
- SalesNexus

- NetSuite
- SugarCRM
- Insightly
- Zoho CRM
- ACT
- Infusionsoft
- ProsperWorks CRM
- Chime
- Maximizer CRM

While there are good choices that could be right for your business, they are not the only tools out there. You can continue your research until you find the solution that you feel best exemplifies what you need for your company.

Biggest CRM Mistakes to Avoid

Using a CRM should be straightforward, but there are still quite a few mistakes that your company could make if they are not careful. Below are some of the biggest mistakes made and ways that you can avoid them.

- **Putting IT in charge** – While it might seem natural for a company to put IT in charge of this system, it should truly be in the hands of sales and marketing. They are going to be using the system most often, and should have input into how it all runs.
- **Not considering the end users** – Always think about the employees who are going to be using the system

when you choose it. Make sure it will meet not only your perceived needs, but their actual needs, as well.

- **Not making sure it fits the company needs** – What does your company really need? If you do not take the time to choose the right CRM, it is going to be a nightmare.

- **Not training employees** – All of the employees who are going to be using the CRM need to have training on how to do so. You cannot just assume everyone will be capable of understanding all the nuances of the system. If you want them to have a good grasp of all of the features and to utilize everything to its fullest, provide them with training.

- **Only thinking about price** – Companies like to save money wherever they can. It is certainly understandable. However, when it comes to choosing the customer relationship management tool you are using for your business, you cannot simply choose the cheaper option. You must find the best choice for your business, even if it does happen to cost a little bit more.

- **No social integration** – With social media being as popular as it is today, it is a mistake not to have social integration in your CRM tool. If you do have it and you are not using it, you are making a mistake.

Content Management Systems

Content management systems, or CMS, help to support the creation of the digital content we've been discussing, as well as the modification of that content. In many cases, there will be a number of users who are working collaboratively on this system as a means to continually create content that will help to improve the company's SEO and their value to visitors.

Many of the CMS available today can help to leverage the visitor information and to create personalized experiences for them. There are many different options when it comes to these types of services including:

- Drupal
- SiteCore
- Magento
- WordPress
- Joomla!
- Wix/Squarespace
- AEM

While these are all CMS options, there are some differences between each of them, and you might find that one would work better for your business than others. You should consider the type of content you are going to create, the number of people who will be working on the team, and the features you believe you will need when you are determining which of these you should consider using. Then, check out each of the options to look at pricing and features.

Digital Asset Management

Digital Asset Management systems, or DAM, will provide you with a place where you can "develop, organize, distribute, and track creative content". This works as something of a library where you can keep all the digital assets you have created. These could include items such as:

- Photos
- Video
- Audio
- Documents
- Images
- Etc.

Once these items are in the library, those who have the clearance are allowed to utilize the items when they are creating content. Some of the newer DAM options will also allow content to be created within the system, if needed.

Being able to manage all of these assets from one location is very convenient, and it can make for a much more effective and efficient use of your resources. You will not have to worry about multiple versions of the content floating around, and you will not have to worry about two different teams creating the same content for their own use.

You can find plenty of great options when you are looking for a DAM such as:

- Webdam
- Northplains
- Canto
- Widen
- Opentext

You will want to take the same approach as when you were looking for a CMS. Determine what you need and then compare and contrast the platforms to see which one will work the best for your company. Ideally, you will want to choose a DAM that can grow along with your business.

Marketing Clouds

Marketing clouds also have the capability to provide users with a wide range of solutions for their marketing needs. One of the benefits of being in "the cloud" is the fact that you can access the items you need no matter where you might be, as long as you have a device that you can connect to the Internet. This means it's possible to work from just about anywhere, so you can stay on top of your marketing when you are out of the office and traveling for business.

Working in the cloud can offer a range of benefits including increased flexibility, disaster recovery, automatic updates to the software, better collaboration, document control, and better security.

When you are choosing from among the various marketing cloud options, you will want to consider the same factors as when you were looking at the marketing platforms in the last section. This will help to ensure you are getting a service that is perfect for your company.

Marketing Cloud Options to Consider

Some of the popular options for marketing clouds include:

- Salesforce Marketing Cloud
- Adobe Marketing Cloud
- IBM Interactive Marketing Solution
- Oracle Marketing Cloud
- AgilOne Predictive Marketing Cloud

Salesforce Marketing Cloud

Salesforce offers up some fantastic features and products for their marketing cloud. They have the Journey Builder, which is designed for 1-to-1 customer journeys through channels such as email, mobile ads, and other areas on the web. It is possible to connect marketing across a range of areas including commerce, sales, and service. They offer email, data collection, a social studio, an advertising studio, a mobile studio, and more.

This service is one of the top options available when it comes to marketing clouds, but it is not the only choice. You will want to check out the others on the list, as well. Find the one that works for you.

Adobe Marketing Cloud

The Adobe Marketing Cloud is another option you might want to consider. This allows for personalization, and it can allow for easy content and asset management, while helping you to increase the engagement of your customers and clients. The goal of this cloud platform is to help you to create a solid foundation for the digital world, and to improve your content across all the channels you use.

You will find plenty to use and enjoy, and it could be an appropriate solution for you.

IBM Interactive Marketing Solution

IBM is one of the most trusted names in the business, and they have some impressive solutions available when it comes to the cloud, and that includes the marketing cloud. Utilize data, analytics, develop and test, scale to your needs, work with mobile, and so much more. It is a secure and popular solution that could have features that will work well for your needs.

Oracle Marketing Cloud

Another great marketing cloud option comes from Oracle. Again, this is a trusted name in the field. They have a range of tools and features designed with the modern marketer in mind. You can work with lead management systems, employ cross channel marketing, personalize the content that you create, automate your marketing and connect with your audience like never before.

AgilOne Predictive Marketing Cloud

AgileOne offers their Predictive Marketing Cloud, which has some nice features, too. It will provide you with customer data from your various channels – both physical and digital. It will help you to analyze and predict the behavior of your customers, which is fantastic for marketers. You can engage with your customers more often and in a meaningful way.

Check for a Free Demo or Trial

When you are choosing a marketing cloud platform, always check to see if they have a free trial or a demo version that you can experience. This provides you with a better look at how it all really works, the features it has, and whether it is the best option for you or not.

Amazon Marketing

Another piece of technology that some companies and marketing teams might want to start utilizing is Amazon Marketing. Amazon, as most are aware, happens to be one of the most prominent websites in the world today. Leveraging marketing power through Amazon might be something you want to consider.

When you use Amazon Marketing Services, it can help you to reach customers and drive sales to the products you offer on the site. If you are selling products, and you offer those products through Amazon, you will want to consider utilizing this option.

If you've been to Amazon, or if you've seen Amazon ads on other sites on the web, you know their distinctive look and style. Amazon is a trusted brand today, so when you work with AMS, you have a sort of built-in trust already working on your side.

AMS allows you to create quality ads quickly and easily. These ads can then be displayed in search results, or on product detail pages. This is a PPC, pay per click, service, so you will only have to pay when a shopper clicks on your ad.

If you have done a good job with the description you've created, then there is a good chance the customer will follow through and buy. Great images, a good price, and a fantastic description, as well as a good seller rating (see below) are essential if you want to do well.

When marketing through Amazon, you will also find detailed reports that show the number of clicks you received, the sales you made, and more. This information can help you with your future sales, as it can help to pinpoint some of the things that you might have done wrong.

For example, if people are not clicking on the ad, you need to reword it or you need to think about your price. If they are clicking on the ad, but they are not buying, you need to consider your description, and make sure you have a good seller rating.

When you are working with Amazon Marketing Services, you will find that you can easily build a campaign and it only takes a few minutes. In addition, you can set the budget at which you are comfortable. In fact, you can begin with a budget that is just $1 a day if you would like.

Keeping a Good Seller Rating

If you are selling through Amazon, you want to do everything you can to keep a stellar seller rating. When people are buying from a company selling on Amazon, it is easy to see the seller rating. A poor rating means most customers are going to pass you by, even if you have the product they want and a good price. They would rather work with a company that can follow through with their promises.

What can you do to help keep a great seller rating on Amazon? One of the first things you must do, painful as it might seem, is to look at the feedback you are getting from the customers. What are the chief complaints they are offering? Do you find that the complaints are the same from multiple customers? Are they isolated incidents?

When a customer has a question, concern, or complaint, and they reach out to you, make sure you answer them satisfactorily. In addition, you will want to answer them as quickly as you can so they are not waiting for answers. Ideally, you will respond to them within 24 hours at most. Always strive to make things right. If there is a problem with your product, do not try to hide it; address it. Make it right, and fix it.

Check your description, too. Make sure the description is accurate when it comes to the product people are getting. Vague or incorrect descriptions can cause customers to think they are getting something else when they buy from you. There are plenty of interesting reviews on Amazon from disgruntled customers who were unaware of the size or style of a product they bought because the description was not accurate.

Some of the other problems customers might have and that might cause them to leave a low seller rating include incorrect orders and issues with the shipping. You can work to make sure the orders are correct, but sometimes shipping is out of your hands. Do your best, but realize that it's not easy to keep a 100% seller rating on any site, much less Amazon.

You Can't Please Everyone

Keep in mind that no matter how hard you might try, you cannot please everyone no matter how hard you try. There will always be those who are going to leave bad reviews or bad seller ratings for one reason or another. Strive to take care of as many problems as possible and keep your customers happy, and you will keep your seller rating in a good place.

What Can You Learn from Amazon?

Why do you want to sell on Amazon? Just look at the success they've had as a selling platform. They are massive, and they offer a range of services. The site and their services have come a long way in the past decades. They tend to have more than a $1 trillion in sales annually. They are the powerhouse when it comes to ecommerce.

What are some of the things that really help Amazon to be the top player when it comes to online selling?

- Pages load quickly
- Personalization
- Easy searching
- Reviews
- Similar products and upselling
- Testing

The site has amazing page speed. When you go to the site, as long as you have a good connection, the pages load with lightning speed. They understand that people want to browse without waiting for pages to load, and they know that people have short attention spans. They will simply go to another site if they have to wait for too long.

When you have an account at Amazon, they personalize the content you see. The site "learns" your likes based on your shopping trends, and then it can recommend items that are specific for you.

Amazon understands that people want a search system that works well, and that can bring them the products, and related products they want to buy, as well as upselling with products that other customers have bought together with the product you are buying. It's a brilliant way to get the customers to find items they want and to get them to make a larger purchase than they initially thought.

Reviews are essential, as well. Some companies are afraid of having reviews on their own sites, or even of having reviews of their products on Amazon. However, if you have a strong product and you believe in that product, you should welcome the reviews. It is true that you will sometimes get bad reviews, deserved or not. If you have a good product though, the good will outweigh the bad.

Think about the way you make most of your purchases. If you have not bought an item before, you want to check out some reviews to see what other people think about the item. The same is true of people who are buying your products. Reviews are essential in today's world.

Amazon understands the power of testing, as well. Sometimes, ads do not work as well as you had hoped. By testing, you can get a better idea of what does and does not work, and you can focus your marketing in those areas.

Tips for Better Amazon Marketing

Do you want to sell more products on Amazon? Of course – every seller does! You can use the following tips to help with your marketing and sales through Amazon.

- You need competitive prices
- Get a pro merchant subscription
- Make your listings unique
- Market to the Amazon customers

People want to get the product for the best price possible, and that is why they come to Amazon. They know the site is renowned for great prices. If you are selling your products for more than the competition, who do you think the customers are going to choose? They are going to buy from the competition most of the time.

You might also want to consider getting a pro merchant subscription, as this can offer you quite a few benefits. The cost is low – less than $40 a month currently.

If you are an individual seller, you will be paying 99 cents per transaction. This might not seem like a lot, but if you are selling a lot through Amazon, that adds up quickly. When you have a pro merchant account, you will not have to pay anything. Those who are selling more than 40 products a month can easily see the benefits.

However, those are certainly not the only benefits from Amazon's pro merchant subscription. You are also able to upload in bulk. Instead of listing the items one at a time, which is time consuming, you can upload a full catalog using APIs, application programming interfaces, or spreadsheet templates. Other benefits include enhanced reporting, more options for selling, and the ability to add unique items to the marketplace.

You should also be sure to make your listing unique so it stands out in the search engines, as well as to people who are buying on Amazon. If they read the same old description from every seller offering the same product, there is nothing that makes them want to buy from you. Unique, well-written descriptions are a great way to capture the attention and imagination of potential customers. A good description might just make them want to buy.

If you are selling through Amazon, it makes sense to market to your Amazon customers. When you make a sale through Amazon, you can target the customer and market to them again. In fact, you can market to them by sending a discount to them for their next purchase. Even a small discount can make them want to buy from your company again, and it brings them into your marketing loop.

eBay Marketing

When you think about online selling, the two companies that tend to come to mind the most are Amazon and eBay. eBay started life as an online auction, and it still offers auctions for a wide range of products. However, the site is no longer just for used items or collectibles sold at auction.

There is plenty of room on this site for all sorts of products, and many companies have started to sell directly through eBay. It was one of the pioneers of ecommerce, and it is still one of the most popular sites on the Internet. The large audience is ready to buy, and they could be looking for products just like yours. When you sell on eBay, it can help to boost your SEO, too.

Why Sell on eBay?

Having multiple outlets online, where you can sell your goods is always important, but what it is that helps to make eBay a great place to sell? As we mentioned, eBay has a large audience of people who are looking for many different types of items. However, that's only one of the reasons to sell on eBay. Let's look at some of the other reasons you might want to start offering your items through the online auction site if you haven't already.

You do not need to have an auction. You can simply post items that you want to sell and have a buy now price. It is a good way to move extra inventory that you have and that you are not selling through other channels. For example, if you have out of season inventory, eBay can be a good place to sell it.

eBay also works to help boost your SEO and your advertising. You can get the word out about your company for minimal cost. You can launch new products, expand and start working with International markets, and more.

It also happens to be easy to get started with eBay, and they have some simple selling tools that can help you with your first sales and to get a hang of the system.

Many small and mid-sized companies are starting to sell directly through eBay as one of their additional channels, and it is working out well for them. It could be a good option for you, as well.

Great eBay Marketing Tips

Do you want to do more than just sell a few products on eBay? Naturally. You want to make the most out of the experience, and here are some great ways to do it.

Many companies are simply looking to sell their items through eBay. They are not thinking about the big picture. What you can do is make sure you have a unique description and educate the buyers when they come to your listing. This helps to differentiate you from other sellers. Let people know about your brand through your product listing to get them interested in your company, not just your product. Add your own voice to the listing, and it can help to set you apart from the competitors who are offering similar products.

You should also work to get as many positive reviews as possible, just as you would when you are working with Amazon. Good reviews help to increase the confidence of other customers when they come to your site. However, you never want to make the egregious error of paying for reviews no matter where they are posted. The reviews need to be honest. Run a good company and have great products and service, and you will find that most of your reviews tend to be good.

Communicate with your customers. When they have problems or questions about a product you are offering, you want to make sure you are answering them as quickly as possible. Again, you can have a window of about 24 hours. More than that, and they will wonder if you are ever going to answer.

Use a quality shipper that it trustworthy and fast, and that offers good prices. If possible, give your customers options on the shipping. For example, if they need to have an item faster, you might want to offer expedited shipping. Customers like to have more options when they are ordering.

As you can see, these are simple, classical tips, but they work. They work for eBay, and they work for other online channels, as well. You do not have to keep searching for a new tool or "secret marketing technique". You can rely on good, solid digital marketing to lead you to success.

Alibaba/AliExpress Marketing

Alibaba is an ecommerce company from China that offers a range of services including consumer to consumer, business to consumer, and business to business sales. They have a quality search engine on the site, as well as cloud computing services. Since 1998, they have grown to become a trusted brand in the ecommerce business, and many sellers and companies are using their services to offer products around the world. They also launched AliExpress, which is for exporters who are in China and who want to reach customers around the world.

It is one of, if not the largest online commerce companies in the world. The Chinese company is responsible for 80% of the online shopping done in China, and in 2017, they will be taking in an estimated $713 billion. Already, they are making more than Amazon and eBay… combined.

The sites are free for users and shoppers, but those who want to sell will have to pay to have their ads stand out on the site. In addition to paying, it is also important to have quality advertisements and descriptions, as well as images, for the products you are trying to sell.

One of the problems that has plagued Alibaba and its sites, which has also affected some of the other online ecommerce platforms, is the proliferation of fakes. Some brands are claiming that some of the items sold through Alibaba are counterfeits and warning people against buying. Alibaba says they spend millions of dollars battling these fakes each year and they respond quickly when there are listings that might be suspect on their site.

By working to take down the fake listings, it helps to foster more confidence in the buyers. China is a fast-growing ecommerce market, and the site is poised to continue doing well in the coming years, and there does not seem to be any shortage of customers. They have users in countries around the world today.

Getting Started

Naturally, most companies will want to consider selling in the market depending on the type of products they are offering. Fortunately, it's easy to get started. You simply go to their site, create an account and let them know if you are a supplier, buyer or both, complete your contact information, and then create your account.

From there, you can start adding product names and keywords, and choose the category for the product so customers can find it. You can then enter product details, images, and the description.

You can also create a company profile stating what type of business you have. Filling out this information completely is always a good idea, as it is another area where you can improve your branding and let people know more about what the company can offer.

Great Listings Help Sell Products

Selling on Alibaba is no different from selling on other sites on the web. There are certain things you must do to make your listing stand out and attract the attention of potential buyers.

It needs to have high quality photos. Blurry photos simply won't do in today's world. The listing also needs to have the right keywords and the right product name and specifications. The descriptions you use should be unique, as well. Just because you are also selling on Amazon or other sites does not mean you should reuse the same description from one site to another. Remember to use your keywords and make it unique.

Marketing and Advertising Tech

When you start to look up the different options available with marketing technology today, you will find an overwhelming number of choices that might be right for your company. Of course, they might not be necessary at all. All those companies – more than a thousand of them – offering marketing tech are trying to market those items to you. Some are useful, but others simply aren't needed.

You want to make sure that you find the items that are needed to improve your marketing platform. Let's look at some of the options you should be using. We'll learn a bit about the type of tech, and some of the options you can use. We've discussed many of these sorts of tools in the book already, so this will be more of a concise rundown of elements you should be using.

- Conversion Optimization Tools
- Email
- Analytics
- Search Engine Marketing
- Remarketing
- Mobile
- Marketing Automation

Conversion Optimization Tools

Conversion optimization is the act of getting people who visit your website to take some form of action. For example, you might want them to become a customer when they come to your site. If it is the first visit, you might want them to sign up for an account or for a newsletter. It could be just about anything, and it typically involves filling out a form of some type.

The average percentage of people who are willing to fill out a form online tends to be around 3%. However, those who are utilizing conversion optimization tools can double this number or even get higher conversions in some cases. You always want to have as many people possible convert, so it might be well worth your while to use one of these tools.

A range of options are available that could help you improve your conversion rate. These include Unbounce, which will help you to create A/B test pages for your landing page. You can determine which one works best and continue to improve your page. Another tool that lets you do this is called Optimizely. If you would like to see how your page stands up to the competition, you can always check out the Landing Page Grader from WordStream. It can provide you with a benchmark page to let you know how your landing page stacks up.

Email

We've mentioned that email marketing can still be a great tool. In fact, it is one of the essential marketing tools that you must employ in the digital age. Building a good list of people who have an actual interest in your product is the best way to create a list of potential customers. Refer to the section on email to find some of the best choices to use with email marketing.

Analytics

Of course, we also need to have methods of tracking everything that's happening with the various marketing outlets. Analytics tools and software are an ideal way to do just that. It is one of the best parts about working in the digital age – there is far less guesswork than there was in the past, and that makes for better and more effective marketing campaigns.

One of the best and most common types of tools to use is Google Analytics. In fact, this is the tool of choice for around 80% of small and mid-sized websites. There is a free version that is quite powerful, and there is a paid version for those who find that they need to have something a bit more. There are other paid options out there, as well, such as Adobe Analytics. You may want to see what they can provide, as well as what other choices have in terms of features, too.

Search Engine Marketing

Search engine marketing, or SEM, is the practice of buying traffic by using paid search listings. It is a common type of marketing, and many companies use this along with SEO to help bring traffic to their site and to increase their sales.

One of the most popular tools used for SEM today is Google AdWords, followed by Bing Ads and Yahoo Search Ads. You've see these SEM ads plenty of times before. Whenever you use a search engine, there are paid results, usually along the top or the side of the search results. This is guaranteed to make sure your ads are seen, and it is a good complement to your SEO work.

Tips to Improve Your SEM

When you work with SEM, you can easily monitor the impressions and clicks you are receiving, but it is important to remember that a successful campaign is about quite a bit more than just the click-through rate, or CTR.

To get more information, you might want to start using tracked links. With these links that go to your original content, you can add unique code to the end of it for each of the channels you are using, such as a paid search engine post, social media post, etc. Since each of these URLs is technically unique, your analytics can then let you see which of the channels you are using is providing you with the best results.

Quality, competitive ad copy is vital, as well. Even though you have just a small space for these types of ads, you will want to make sure that you are using the most of that space. Write ads specific to the keywords you are using, and cater ad copy to the buyer needs. Remember, you should know who your buyers are and what they want by now. Write the copy directed at them. Test different ads to see which one works best for you.

The copy you use should carry over to the landing page if possible, as the continuity can help to carry the reader through the page and improve conversion rates. When it comes to the landing page, you want to make sure it is clean, clear and as easy as possible to navigate. Break the text up into readable chunks and let people know what the page is about right away. If people can't find the information they need right away, they are going to click off the page, and that's a wasted opportunity.

The page should also make it easy for the person to convert; whether signing up for a newsletter or buying a product. If it makes sense for your offerings, having a "Buy Now" button, or a "Sign Up Now" button that's large and easy to see could be a good idea.

One of the other things you need to consider when designing the landing page is the fact that many of your users will be visiting from their mobile devices. You need to make your pages mobile friendly so they are still easy to read and navigate.

Always be sure to track your campaign results, as well, so you can find out what works and what doesn't. It then becomes easier to improve your next marketing campaign. You might find that you have the best results with Google Ads, for example. Others might do better with Bing or another option, such as advertising through social media channels like Facebook.

Find out what works best for your company and remember to always keep testing your ads.

Remarketing

The term remarketing is to refer to strategies and techniques used by sellers and marketers to follow up with visitors who did not take a desired action when they arrived at the website. For example, if someone abandons their shopping cart on a site, meaning they click off the site and decide not to buy, remarketing would be following up and attempting to bring the visitor back to the site. This is generally done through an automated email system.

REMARKETING CAMPAIGNS
Don't lose your visitors forever...

Prospect → Visits your site → Prospect is tracked → Prospect leaves your site → Your ad on another site

Prospect returns to your site

Image 20-Source ID: A20

If the customer is already set up and registered on your site with their email, it becomes easy to remarket to them. The goal of remarketing is to convert the visitor into a paying customer.

Some other terms have cropped up that mean essentially the same thing – conversion marketing and cart abandonment email marketing. The remarketing effort should aim to do more than just get the customer back to the shopping cart. It should take steps to nurture the relationship between the potential customer and your business. Make them feel important and show them how your product or services can help.

CONTENT VS. PRODUCT RETARGET

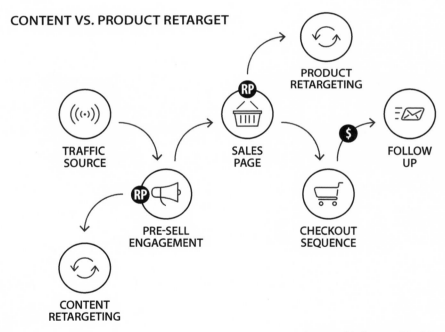

Image 21-Source ID: A21

Mobile

In recent years, mobile technology has truly changed the way people interact with the Internet. Most people have smartphones with them all the time, which means they are always connected to the web. Therefore, marketers need to consider how to best use this mobile technology to their advantage.

Making mobile friendly sites, as we've mentioned, is essential. People will usually have access to their email through their mobile devices, as well, so even email marketing can be targeted to mobile users, as can SMS and MMS marketing.

App based marketing and in-game mobile marketing can work for some companies, as well. Keep in mind that today, there is quite a bit of competition in these fields, but it could still work. Having an app that allows the users to connect to your site, offers discounts, or has other ways for them to connect with your company can help to foster and increase brand loyalty.

However, apps may not be appropriate for all types of companies, and you have to weigh the benefits against the cost of creating and maintaining the application.

Look for Other Tools and Tech to Help With Advertising and Marketing

Are there other types of tools out there that might be able to help your marketing efforts? Sure, and you might eventually want to integrate some of those for your marketing team. Just make sure you are using items that are truly going to make a positive difference to your marketing and that they are not overly difficult to implement.

Language Tech

Language technology, sometimes called human language technology, or HLT, has entered the technical and digital realm, as well, and there are even some ways it can be used for marketing. Today, researchers are trying to "teach" computers to understand language. Naturally, this is one of the biggest hurdles that will be faced when it comes to artificial intelligence simply because of the complexities of language.

Natural language processing technology, NLP, can use grammatical or linguistic combined with machine learning techniques. They are making strides in this field, and it has the potential to become a large industry. It can also be beneficial in the field of ecommerce and marketing.

One of the ways marketers are utilizing language technology today is to analyze social media. They can look for the volume of mentions and the sentiment of those mentions as long as the data is calibrated on the expected reach and also includes demographic info. It helps with social segmentation, which can allow for better, targeted campaigns.

The technology can scour social sites, surveys, and the like to find what is called propensity statements. This can let marketers know who might be thinking about purchasing a product, going on a vacation, eating out, etc. Then, the marketer can target those people to help match them with appropriate items.

Analyzing email campaign messages can show what element of an email message was most effective for the users. This allows better, more targeted emails to be created in the future, which can make the emails appear to be more personal.

Implementing Language Technology

NLP as a service is still relatively new, but there are companies emerging who can help companies interested in taking advantage of this field. It is also possible to find a range of APIs that you could use including Skyttle 2.0. This tool can extract keywords and keyword phrases that are topical, as well as gauging whether the context and sentiment is positive or negative. The tool currently supports English, French, German, and Russian.

Pros and Cons for Proxy vs. CMS Integration Paths to Your Spanish Language Website

Let's look further into language technology options, so you can find the solution that will work best for your site. Both proxy and CMS can help you and your staff to save countless hours of preparation, and both can retain strong branding, style, and navigation to ensure a quality site for other languages.

Translation Proxy Advantages

Those who have smaller companies and websites that are relatively simple will find that proxy technology can do a good job. It is easy to set up and then just walk away. While this was a popular option between five and ten years ago, it is falling out of popularity today, but it can still be used. There is a minimal amount of commitment and involvement from the staff, which is nice for those companies that simply do not have enough staff to manage and control CMS platforms.

Translation Proxy Disadvantages

Of course, even though there are some advantages to using a proxy, you also need to consider some of the disadvantages, as well. This is an all or none choice. You will have to send all for Spanish, or send none, and you may find that there is still some bleed through of English on the site. This can be jarring for someone who is reading the site in Spanish and who suddenly finds some words in English. Naturally, this provides the customers with a less than optimal experience.

For large companies, security can also be more of an issue with a proxy service. They do not do well with dynamic web pages, and it can be very difficult to use for sites that have scripting for things such as shopping carts, comments, filtering, and search. Even if there are small changes to the source site after logging in, it can essentially break the proxy implementation. This will cause issues with the content and the layout.

If you then try to work with additional language, it reduces the amount of control you have. Trying to keep a solid look for the style, or even continuity in the content, can be difficult. This is true whether you are making large or small changes. Of course, this also causes issues with your SEO, as it can be difficult to get the relevant keywords for your site in all of these various languages. For some companies, this simply presents too much of a challenge or hassle.

Those who are considering utilizing language technology for their company have to consider a range of factors before using it. They should consider what languages they need supported, how easy or difficult it will be to implement the technology into their existing infrastructure, and whether the technology will be able to scale with the company.

CMS Integration Advantages

When you utilize CMS, you will have more control and a greater ability to plan with the teams working on branding and content. This way, you can only translate certain pages if you want, and you do not need to send the entire set of pages for translation. There is no need for firewall openings either.

The CMS integration can provide a simpler experience for the users, making it easy to create content, change images, and create workflow models as needed. It can provide better consistency throughout, and it can make for a more efficient and cost saving experience overall.

CMS Integration Disadvantages

The disadvantages here are quite minimal, thankfully. The staff will still need to control and manage the structure of the website. In addition, when you first start with this integration, you will find that it does take some time to set up the workflows mentioned earlier and to test them to make sure they are working properly. Once this is complete, however, things should flow quite smoothly.

SoLoMo

SoLoMo is not the latest and greatest neighborhood in New York City. It stands for Social, Local and Mobile marketing. We've discussed social marketing in detail in Chapter 8, so we will learn more about ways you can use and improve local and mobile marketing in this section.

SO-LO-MO

SOCIAL   **LOCAL**   **MOBILE**

Image 22-Source ID: A22

Local Marketing

When people are searching the web on their phone, there is a good chance they are looking for something that is local. People who perform what they consider to be a successful search often visit that store or establishment within the same day or within a couple of days.

Local marketing therefore revolves around a local service or local establishment. It does not apply to those who are digital only, as there is no need for a local focus. Marketing efforts for the local services and establishments need to be focused on bringing customers through the doors.

While it is still advisable to use some traditional marketing tactics that you have used in the past, such as having local events or even street teams, working with all of the digital technology available is also important.

Digital tools can be a huge benefit, and you will find that they also tend to be easy to implement. Keep in mind that the local marketing we discuss here can and should be combined with social and mobile. Ideally, they will all work together.

Online Directories

An online directory can be extremely helpful for local marketing, and it is one of the first steps you want to take. Check out listings, such as Yahoo Business Listings, Google My Business, and Bing Places for Business, as well as any others you find. Many options are out there, and they are free to use. It just takes some time and a little effort to fill them out.

Fill out your business information fully, and it can then help your rankings. When people are looking for your business, or a business like yours, it is likely to come up in their local search results.

Local SEO

You should also be thinking about the search words and phrases you are using. If you want to show up higher in the search results locally, then you want to localize your SEO. This is very simple to do. You add local terms, such as your city and even neighborhood locations to the content you are creating. Let's look at a very simplified example to give you an idea of how this would work. Instead of merely having the phrase "best burgers", if you were in the Bronx, you might use "best burgers in the Bronx".

You want to make sure your operating area is in the keywords on all of your pages and title fields, and even backlinks when possible. Use local search terms for your video descriptions, images, and in social media posts. All the local terms will eventually help your business to rise in the rankings when people are searching for those products or services in your area.

The utilization of GPS, geofencing, and RFID can help to drive even more conversions through location-based coupons, promotions, and other types of offers. Many who are on mobile find that location-based coupons are very useful, and that they are quite welcome.

Geofencing is essentially a virtual perimeter in the real world. It allows for certain actions to occur for those who are within this perimeter, such as sending them offers. There are three types of action triggers for geofencing. They include:

- **Static** – This is based on the person's position to a certain area. For example, they might get a text message with a coupon in it when they enter a store that is using this technology.

- **Dynamic** – This is based on a changing data stream and the user's relative position to that stream. A common example used would be to let someone know of an open parking space via notifications when they are driving through certain areas.

- **Peer-to-peer** – These occur when a user is in proximity to others who are using a social app. For example, check-in notifications from friends who are using Facebook.

Both app-based and network-based geofences are available. The app-based geofences utilize a mobile app that will share the user's locational data through GPS. Any business that wants to use this option will need to have a mobile app up and ready to go first, and then have it listed on the app stores so customers can download it. For this to work the app needs to be running and the location services need to be enabled.

For the network-based geofence, it utilizes data from cell phone towers to send messages to mobile users connected to the network. This is on an opt-in basis, so the customers do not become overwhelmed with messages. You could get the customers to opt for this service by having them fill out a form on your site or scan a QR code, for example. One of the big advantages to this is the fact that you will not have to develop a mobile app, which can help to reduce the company's costs.

Great Design

Local marketing is going to benefit from having high quality design just as much as any other form of digital marketing. Make sure your site is clean and clear and easy to navigate. Be sure local customers can find the information that it likely to be most important to them.

The directions to your physical store, your hours, parking information, and the like are generally going to be elements that people want to know. Allow the users to map their route to your location right from your site to make it easy for them. You might also want to have a call button on your site, so they can get in touch with you if needed. Whatever page they might happen to land on, based on the link they clicked, needs to be relevant and provide them with the information they would expect.

Call to Action

Never forget to add a call to action to your pages. When the potential customer is reading the page, you want to urge them to do something. A clear call to action will help the visitors to understand exactly what they should do next, and it can help to reduce the bounce rates from your site. Maybe you tell them to call for an appointment, send an email, or visit now; make sure the call is clear and simple.

Customer Value Proposition

What is it that makes your business better than the rest of the local competition? As always, you need to make sure you are clear with your customer value proposition, or CVP. This is the term for the benefits provided to those who convert and become customers. Whether local, national, or international, marketing should be clear about what you can do for the customers and why your company is a better choice than the competition.

If you can't wow them with the CVP, and then with the final product or service, they are not going to want to do business with you.

Mobile Marketing

Mobile marketing does well when used in conjunction with social marketing and local marketing. It is just as important as the other elements of the SoLoMo triad. Just because you have a website or blog that shows up in the search results when someone is on a mobile device, it does not mean that you are ready for mobile. It is important to have a mobile-friendly version of your site that is optimized for all devices so everyone can have a good experience when they visit. If it's frustrating or hard to navigate, they are going to leave. You can't blame them. It's the same thing you would do if you came to a site that was difficult to use.

You can also consider developing an app, as we mentioned earlier. Just remember the precautions and make sure it is the right choice for your company.

Make it possible for customers and potential customers to sign up for alerts and messages from your business, as well. You can send timely marketing right to their phone and provide them with a special of some type, or let them know about a limited offer.

However, you need to make sure you do not overdo it with the SMS messages, even when they have allowed you to send them to their mobile device. Sending too many will be seen as spam, and they are going to rescind the right to send messages.

Start out slowly with just one or two per month, and see how the customers are responding. You can slowly add one or two more per month, but it is always better to err on the side of caution and keep customers happy rather than inundate them and cause them to leave.

Make Them Work Together

Remember to make sure all of these various elements are working together in your marketing campaign. Local should support mobile and social and vice versa. This is the best way to find success. Focusing only on certain areas can limit your ability to provide marketing messages the customers will see, want, and use. This does not mean you need to use all of the tools we've discussed in the book. However, it does mean you need to hit all of the different digital avenues – social, local, mobile, website, blog, etc. – that we have covered. Make them work together in the POINTS system for the best results.

Software Review Sites

Take a moment to consider the tools we've mentioned and discussed in the book thus far. With all of the options available, finding just the right one can prove to be difficult. That's where software review sites can be a help.

These sites often gather similar types of software meant to help with a certain area of business, marketing in our case. They will then review, and sometimes rank, the offerings. This can provide you with a handy list of some of the best options.

Of course, there are some problems with software review sites, too. The criteria on which they base parts of the review might not be as important to you. There could be parts of the software that they have glossed over or not looked at in the review. Always read the reviews to see what is and is not mentioned to help give you a better idea of what the software can truly do.

At the end of the day, reviews are opinions. It is important to find opinions that are trustworthy. You want to make sure you are putting your faith in sites that have developed a good reputation for providing thorough and honest reviews.

Trust in Quality Sites

What are some of the best software review sites? Many quality sites are up and running today, but you want to be diligent about those you choose to follow. If you notice that the sites are doing nothing but praising all of the software they are reviewing, it could mean they are actually affiliates getting money from the software they are reviewing and trying to convince people to buy. This does not mean you can't trust a review on an affiliate site. However, it does mean you shouldn't only rely on sites from affiliates to make your decision. You also want to look at reviews from unbiased, third party sites.

Some of the sites you might want to consider include:

- TopTenReviews.com
- CNET.com
- SoftwareReviews.com
- TomsGuide.com
- SoftwareAdvice.com

Keep in mind that these are just some of the review sites. You will find plenty of others once you start looking at specific types of marketing sites. These tend to be some of the most trusted sites available, though.

Good review sites tend to provide information on the features of the software, as well as whether it is cloud-based or location-based. They may also have the price available, the platforms it works with, such as Windows, Mac, and Linux, and whether it is best for a small, medium, or large-sized company. Some will also have ratings and reviews from actual customers.

Check for User Reviews

In addition to looking at sites for reviews of the software and platforms you are considering, it is also a good idea to consider checking some reviews from actual users. These are other professionals who have bought and used the software in a real-world setting regularly.

One of the nice things about reviews from people who use the software regularly is that they can more readily tell you the good and bad things about the software that might not be evident in a short review on a site.

Remember to Try Demos

Many of the types of software marketers will use can be expensive. You do not want to make a mistake and buy into software that does not offer the features you need or that will not integrate well with other software you are already using. This will only cause further costs down the road as you have to replace the software. Therefore, if a piece of software offers a demo or a trial, and most do, you should take advantage of it.

When you try the demos, be sure to put it through its paces and try out everything you could possibly need. If it is unclear whether it will integrate into your system, make sure you ask one of the representatives from the company. You would expect your own customers to ask questions of your sales reps to make sure the product or service is right for them. You should do the same thing when you are choosing a piece of software for your company.

APIs and Connectors

Integration can be a difficult concept to understand, and sometimes, it is best if you have an IT department that can help to build integrations into your company. However, whether you take care of it on your own or have outside help, you will want to understand what APIs, connectors and integration applications are.

An API is an application programming interface, and it is a way to access information using the system functionality instead of the user interface. The APIs are often used by those who are not happy with the UI that comes with the software. The API can "plug into" the software digitally and create another way for the user to interface with it, which may be more in line with what the user truly needs. Some of the APIs might add additional functionality, as well.

A connector is literally the device that connects from the "point of references to the destination system". It can allow for the interactivity that needs to take place between the software and the API. The connectors can often support different types of functionality. A common example is using physical connectors that most can understand is an HDMI slot that can handle both sound and video.

The connectors are often categorized by the protocol they support, or the type of system they can connect to. Some of the common types of connectors you might see include:

- JDBC Connectors
- .NET Connectors
- HTTP Connectors
- Salesforce Connectors
- SAP Connectors

Integration applications will usually have multiple connectors, which can then gather information from APIs, modify and change the mapping data and information, and more. Multiple types of software can be put together in the same setup, and the integration applications act as middleware to make sure everything works together across the enterprise.

EAI, or enterprise application integration, it the term used for the plans and tools being brought into a company to ensure all of the software and apps are working together. Depending on the size and complexity of the software and apps you are using, and want to add, to the company, this has the potential to be difficult unless you have some help.

For many who are in marketing and related fields, it can still be difficult to understand how best to use these in your own system and how to perform all of the behind the scenes work that gets everything to work well together. This can be frustrating. Those who have questions can connect with their IT department, or an outside specialist for help. This will ensure that everything is working well and that it is working together.

Technology Won't Stop Advancing – Neither Can You

In this chapter, we've discussed quite a few interesting technologies used in marketing and advertising today, as well as how you can work with them and improve your marketing plan. One of the essential things to remember is that technology is only going to keep advancing faster and faster.

New pieces of software, new ways to interact with the Internet, and new ways to market are going to keep coming. Rather than pretending things are always going to stay just the way they are right now, you need to be ready and willing to adopt, learn, and work with new tech when it becomes viable for marketing.

Just look at social media; 25 years ago, few would have been able to predict what a game changer it would be for the Internet, marketing, and the world. Keep up with the changes so you are not left behind.

Notes

If you are following the POINTS Methodology thus far, by the end of this chapter, you should have determined what types of technology stacks you are using to help manage, control, and streamline the marketing ecosystem customer lifecycle flow.

You know that it takes a certain amount of speed and control to succeed in the digital world. If you were to try to handle all your contacts, leads, prospects, and clients without using the proper technology, it will lead to a terrible customer experience. Make sure that you have good, working technology as a part of your organization.

CHAPTER 11

Sustainment

"We should no longer be talking about 'digital marketing' but marketing in a digital world."

– Keith Weed, Unilever

Now that you have a better idea of the actions you need to take and the tools you will need to use, you want to keep things going. You need to make sure you can sustain your marketing campaigns and plans, and improve them for even better results. That brings us to the "S" in the POINTS Method. It's time to learn how you can sustain your momentum and even build some more.

Your Company

What about your company? Do you have enough people to fulfill all of these roles, or is it only a handful of you working on the marketing department? If you happen to have a smaller team, you can always reconfigure the roles so other people can cover other tasks that need to get done. For example, the vice president and the marketing manager might actually be just a single role in some companies.

When you are organizing the company, remember the importance of having well-defined roles for everyone involved. When all staff members know what they are supposed to be doing, the entire system will run far more smoothly. Figure out a system that works for your company now. If you eventually find that you have more employees in the marketing department, you can rework the roles, as needed.

Mapping Current Teams and Roles

ERP, enterprise resource planning, has many parts, and one of the most important steps is called role mapping, which is often followed up by team mapping. This type of mapping or charting refers to several things. It can refer to assigning roles within the software and platforms you are going to be using, including security clearance in the software.

Assigning Roles for Software and Security

You will need to assign those who are going to be using the software their specific roles and make sure they have the security clearance to access all of the tools they need to have for their job. It can be tempting to just give everyone in the company who will be working with the software access to everything. However, that is not a good idea for several reasons.

Allowing everyone access to everything opens up more potential for problems. If someone has too much access to various areas of the software and infrastructure that's been set up, it increases the risk of the information and data in the system. Someone who is unhappy with his or her job, or someone who knows he or she is about to get fired, can wreak havoc. You want to limit the damage that can be done as much as possible. The same is true if one of the employee's information is taken and someone from the outside gets into the system.

Assigning Position and Team Roles

It can also refer to an individual's role, as well as a team's role, within a company. In some organizations, it can be unclear exactly who is supposed to be handling different jobs. This is true of marketing as much as it is other departments. This can cause some people to see others as not doing their jobs, or even see people as encroaching on jobs that are not theirs.

If an individual or a team does not have a clear role within the department, it can lead to duplication of certain tasks or some things will simply never get done. When you have a role map or a role chart, everyone at the company knows and understands exactly what he or she is supposed to be doing. There is no more confusion.

This ensures that all of the various tasks within the department have someone handling them, and that all of the projects are being worked on by a team that knows what it is doing. The marketing managers will have an easier time keeping track of everything that's happening to make sure work is being completed on time.

Imagine just how chaotic and wasteful it could be if even just a couple people are not clear on their roles. Taking the time to assign everyone to the role for which they are best suited makes a big difference. Recruiting the right people in the first place can be beneficial, as well.

Of course, role mapping is about more than just individuals. You also have to make sure the teams, and the "sub" teams within an organization all know their role. For example, the sales department, customer service department, and the marketing department all need to know what their duties encompass. The marketing department might have multiple smaller teams assigned to different projects, too. These would be the sub teams. The departments and teams can work together, but they should never step over their bounds. If there are questions or concerns, they need to know how to contact people in the other departments to let them know about an issue rather than trying to handle a problem on their own. Having clearly defined roles mapped out is one of the best ways to do this.

Recruiting Tools

The goal is to always have the right people working for your organization and in the marketing department. A great team can accomplish just about anything when they put their mind to it. However, creating that team can be something of a problem for many companies. They do not put as much effort into their recruitment processes as they should.

Recruiting Tips to Start Using

It might seem relatively easy to build a good team. You know what you want out of an employee, and then you just have to start the interview process to find a few people that might fit the bill. Of course, it is not truly quite that easy. The hiring process can be quite a bit more difficult, and if you hire the wrong people, it could cost your company substantially.

The best way to make sure you are getting great recruits is to improve the candidate pool even before you start the interview process. You might want to work with professional recruiters, who can take care of some of the legwork for you. Just make sure they are fully aware of exactly what you need from an employee.

You can also ask your current employees if they know anyone who would fit the bill and be interested in the job. The employees know what the job entails, and they might be able to help you find some truly great recruits. Look to professional association websites and magazines when you are advertising for your jobs. You can also consider in-house candidates who might want to work in a different department.

For example, someone in the sales department might want to become a part of the marketing team. This could be a boon, as they might have some insight about the customers that they can bring to the rest of the team.

Be very clear about what the employees' responsibilities and roles will be, and the type of experience and education you require. This can help to weed out those who do not qualify. To be sure, you will still have several candidates who submit their resume everywhere and who you will have to weed out on your own.

Do not skimp on the background checks. Make sure they have the skills, education, and experience they need for the job. References are essential if you hope to hire a great employee. If they are putting egregious lies on their resume, you cannot trust them to become a part of your team. By becoming known as a great employer and offering a good salary, as well as benefits, it can help you to attract a better level of employee.

Hire smart people who will get on well with the team you have in place. Have high standards and make sure the recruits can live up to them long before you offer them a job.

Hiring the Wrong People

If you hire the wrong people, they are not going to last. They might not fit in with the rest of the team. They might not be willing or capable of doing the job. Eventually, they will need to be let go from the company. This means you have wasted time and money training these people. It all goes out the window.

Productivity is sure to suffer, as is the morale of the other employees on the team. If you hire the wrong people, the rest of the team might have to work harder to cover for the poor-quality employee, and this will not sit well with them. Many times, these "bad hires" do not get along with the other employees, and this can cause some serious friction on the team.

The costs associated with hiring the wrong people include separation pay, recruiting fees, advertising for recruits, background checks testing, orientation materials and training programs, onboarding, separation processing, resume screening, and much more.

Check out the poor recruiting habits below to make sure you do not fall into this category.

Poor Recruiting Habits to Avoid

While the tips above can help you to winnow down your choices to the best options from the stable of recruits, you also have to consider some of the problems that come from bad habits that you might have picked up as a recruiter. You will want to watch for the bad habits discussed here to make sure that you are not making them.

When recruiting, you want to make sure you are listening to what the recruits are saying. Too often, recruiters focus on the information they are telling the recruits and they are not listening to what those potential employees are saying. Recruiting the right people is about listening and talking. Often, you can learn quite a bit more when you listen to what people are saying. Keep the interviews relaxed, listen carefully and observe behavior. When you listen and learn, it often becomes clear whether or not they will be a good fit for your team.

Recruiters also need to know exactly what they are looking for when they are bringing someone aboard. In some companies, the HR department is responsible for the hiring process, and they have only some vague guidelines that they use when choosing candidates. They may not know the team or department they are hiring for very well, and they could end up hiring based only on data rather than considering the person behind the resume. Even for those who are hiring for their own department, they may not always know exactly what they are looking for in a recruit. The "ideal recruit" should be created before you start the hiring process. You are looking for someone who can fill that role as closely as possible.

What Recruiting Tools Can Help?

Fortunately, the digital age has also helped to make recruiting a bit easier thanks to some of the tools available. From the various websites where you can place ads to software to help with the recruiting process, there are tools that can help with just about every step in the process of finding the ideal recruit.

In the past, you might have utilized a job board to help find people who might work well in your company. Today, the job boards are digital for the most part. One of the best places to look for recruits is LinkedIn. This is the social media site for professionals to connect with one another. You can learn quite a bit about candidates, and it makes it much easier to find people to whom you can reach out.

You can also utilize video to help you find the best recruits. Make videos about your company and the departments for which you are hiring. Showcase what it is like to work for your company and what type of people are already employed there. You are essentially using your marketing prowess to market your company to potential recruits. The videos should help to give them a better idea of whether or not they will fit well with your company. On the other side of things, you could even have some candidates provide you with an initial video resume.

Checking Social Media

This is something of a controversial area, but it is a practice in which many recruiters engage. They look at the social media pages of potential employees to get a better sense of who they are as people and whether they might be a good fit for the company. Still, this is a slippery slope, and there are people who have some vastly different opinions on whether or not this is right.

Organizational Design

Within the larger organization or company for which you are working, you will also need to consider the organizational design and structure of the marketing department. The design of your marketing organization will often depend on the size of the company. Those who are a part of a small company might only have one or two employees working in marketing. However, a larger company may have scores of employees, and in those cases, a deeper level of organizational structure is required.

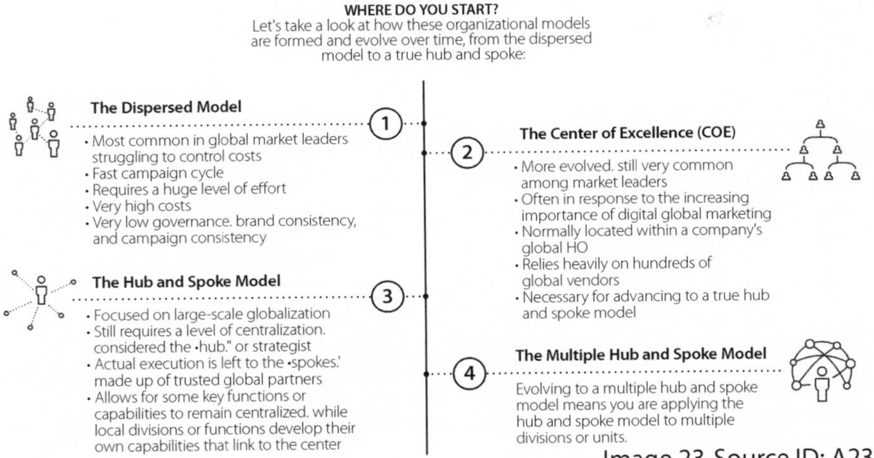

WHERE DO YOU START?
Let's take a look at how these organizational models are formed and evolve over time, from the dispersed model to a true hub and spoke:

The Dispersed Model
1
- Most common in global market leaders struggling to control costs
- Fast campaign cycle
- Requires a huge level of effort
- Very high costs
- Very low governance, brand consistency, and campaign consistency

The Center of Excellence (COE)
2
- More evolved, still very common among market leaders
- Often in response to the increasing importance of digital global marketing
- Normally located within a company's global HO
- Relies heavily on hundreds of global vendors
- Necessary for advancing to a true hub and spoke model

The Hub and Spoke Model
3
- Focused on large-scale globalization
- Still requires a level of centralization, considered the •hub." or strategist
- Actual execution is left to the •spokes.' made up of trusted global partners
- Allows for some key functions or capabilities to remain centralized, while local divisions or functions develop their own capabilities that link to the center

The Multiple Hub and Spoke Model
4
Evolving to a multiple hub and spoke model means you are applying the hub and spoke model to multiple divisions or units.

Image 23-Source ID: A23

Budgeting

When many are first getting into business, they put a substantial amount of their budget into the products they are developing, or the equipment they need on hand to perform their specialized services. While it is good to have a focus on products and services to make sure they are as good as they can possibly be, you cannot neglect budgeting for marketing. In fact, you will quickly find that marketing is going to take up a large chunk of your budget.

What Needs to Be in the Budget?

As you should have already gleaned from the other information in this book, marketing is about more than just direct mail and other types of traditional advertising. You have to consider all of the digital methods that we've discussed.

To help you create a budget, you should first write down a list of all of the various segments you have in your marketing plan. This will include things such as your website, blog upkeep, social media efforts, online advertising, videos, e-books, tracking, and the other elements we've discussed. Write down the platform you plan to use for automation, as well, as you have to factor this into your cost.

Once you have a list of everything that is going into your marketing plan, including the tools and the work to keep the plans running and updated, you need to get an idea of the costs.

Keep in mind that some of the items that are in the budget will be one-time purchases, while others will be recurring. When you are creating the budget, make sure you note not only the price, but also whether it is a recurring cost or a single cost. When do the recurring charges occur?

You also have to estimate the cost of testing different strategies for marketing. This can include things such as coupons and discounts, product giveaways, creating alternate versions of products (different colors, for example), and even working with focus groups.

How do the employees fit into your budget? Are the employees that you hire and make a part of the marketing team considered a part of the budget, or are they separate? If they are considered a part of the budget, this can eat up a lot of money rather quickly. In addition to the salaries, you also have to think about benefits, as well as onboarding costs. This is one of the reasons we talked about recruiting earlier. If you want to keep your costs down, be sure to hire the right people for the job.

The communications campaign – social media, ads, blogs, websites, and offline marketing – is one of the ongoing costs that you need to put into your budget. For many companies, this will be where they end up spending the bulk of their marketing budget, but this can vary from one company to another.

Remember to factor in the monitoring costs, too. This could be included with the marketing or website platforms that you choose, or even through Google Analytics. However, you may want to look into a third-party option that offers more in terms of features, which will add to your budget.

Once the list is complete, you need to add up the costs. Remember, it's a good idea to separate the one-time costs from the recurring costs, so you can get an accurate number of how much you will have to spend.

If you find that your marketing budget appears as if it is going to be too much, look at all of the areas where you are considering spending right now and see where you might be able to cut back. For example, if you are thinking about spending on traditional advertising for print or radio, you should rethink it. After all, this book has proven that digital is a smarter option where you can find more people. It also happens to be cheaper. Find ways that you can cut down the budget so that it can still work for you. Just make sure you are not trimming away any of the essentials we discussed.

What's the Magic Percentage Number?

If you are looking for a quick and easy way to determine the exact percentage you should be spending on your marketing budget, this isn't the place to find it. In fact, there is no magic marketing percentage that is going to work equally well for all companies. For example, VTLDesign.com found that Microsoft spends about 18% of their budget on marketing. SalesForce.com spends 53% of their budget and Apple is only spending 7% of their budget on marketing.

However, the average amount spent by companies is around 10%, and there are some other general rules of thumb that you could follow until you get your footing and know what's right for you. You might want to start out spending 10% of your budget on marketing and then adjust the numbers from there.

Another option is the "rule of thumb" for businesses that are making at least six figures. You can multiply your total revenue by 5% to determine how much you should have for a budget that will maintain the company's current awareness and visibility. If you want to grow and gain customers in the market, you would take your total revenue and then multiply it by 10%.

As mentioned, though, there are no hard and fast rules that will work for everyone when it comes to budgeting for advertising.

Vendor Management

Companies must also make sure they are working to build strong relationships with the vendors they are using, including suppliers. Vendor management is essential, and this can sometimes fall to the marketing team depending on the vendors. It is important to remember that this type of management is not merely about trying to get the lowest price for goods, software, or services that you might be using.

Instead, this is about developing good relationships with the vendors so it is easier to come to agreements with one another that can benefit both companies. When you focus only on getting the lowest price, you will find that most of the vendors are not going to look forward to meeting with you and working with you. They do not see any advantage for them and their company.

Tips for Vendor Management

Make sure you are providing your vendors with information that they need to help serve your needs better. This doesn't mean you have to share trade secrets with them, of course, but you do want to make sure they are aware of things such as design changes, expansion, changes of location, or new product launches. When you keep them in the loop, they tend to keep you in the loop, as well.

You should show that you are committed to the vendor, just as they should be committed to you. However, this does not mean you always take their offer. You should always be on the lookout for new and lower bids. If you find a lower bid, you should let your vendor know and give them an offer to counter or explain why what they offer is better. Even though you develop a relationship with vendors, they still realize that this is all business.

Try to learn more about the vendor's business, just as they are learning about yours. When you do, it can provide you with some more insight into just what they are doing and why certain things may cost what they do. Trying to understand more about what they do can also help you to develop a stronger relationship.

This can also help you to remain flexible with the vendor in certain instances. Just remember that being flexible should never mean bending over backwards for them. They should in turn be flexible with you, such as not having long-term contracts that are restrictive, for example.

Always monitor the performance of the vendor to make sure everything is going according to plan. Just because you have a plan in place does not mean that the plan is always going to go smoothly and that the vendor will perform as expected. By monitoring them, you will know when things go wrong and when you may have to get into touch with the vendor.

Regular communication that is open and honest can go a long way in making sure you have a good relationship with the vendor now and into the future. Ideally, you will try to build partnerships for the long-term so you can grow together into larger and stronger companies.

What Partners Do You Need Now?

Now that you have set up a marketing team and program that you hope is truly sustainable and effective, you should have some key partners in place. These can be the vendors with whom you've already worked, as well as other companies that you would like to partner with for cross-promotion and advertising. You should also be partnering and working closely with the other teams in your company, such as the sales team and the customer service team.

Choosing Partners

The partners that one company needs going forward will be vastly different from other companies. You might still want to consider partnering up with more brands, who are working in similar fields, but who are not direct competitors.

If you do decide to partner up with other brands, always make sure you are clear about your business so they understand who you are and what you do. This will give them a chance to see whether or not they might want to partner with you. Ask questions about the other brand, and encourage them to ask questions about your company. Make sure you understand what you can do for one another that can help both of you to increase your business. If only you will benefit, there are not likely to be many brands jumping at the chance to partner with you.

You must also always be clear about any financial arrangements made, and it is essential to have contracts. The last thing you want to do is get into legal drama with another brand over a misunderstanding.

You might also want to look for some other advertising partners. Once you have started to establish your company more, you might find there are more people who are willing to be celebrity sponsors for the company. Just make sure you refer to that section of the book so you understand how it works and how to stay on the right side of the law.

Maslow's Hierarchy Applied to Employee Engagement

The Hierarchy of Needs comes from Abraham Maslow. He was an American psychologist who believed that the psychological health of someone depended on fulfilling a certain set of needs in order of priority. The theory is that humans, employees in this case, need to have certain basic needs met before they can move ahead and grow, or become engaged. He has set them up like a pyramid. We will go through each of them so you can see how they apply to employees.

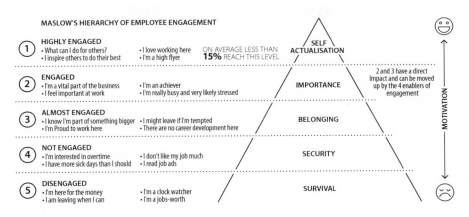

Image 24-Source ID: A24

Survival

At the bottom of the pyramid is the Survival level. At this level, a person's needs are very basic and biological. They include food, water, shelter, and a place to sleep. When it comes to employee engagement, those who are at this level are said to be disengaged. They might have their basic needs covered for employment – they have a job that can pay the bills, and they may have a sense of financial independence. However, that doesn't mean they like what they do.

Someone at this level is not excited by their job and they are only there for the paycheck it provides. They plan to leave when they can and find a new job. They watch the clock and are only biding their time until they can find something that they feel is better.

Security

The next level is security. People who have jobs want to know that those jobs are secure, and many people find it difficult to move past this level of Maslow's Hierarchy due to the nature of the job market today. People want to have some semblance of structure in the workplace, and at this level they might still not have it.

The employees at this level of the hierarchy are somewhat more engaged than those who are stuck in the survival level, but not by much. These employees are generally not interested in doing any overtime, and they will often refuse it. They are not happy with their working conditions in some cases, and in other cases, they might not get along well with their coworkers or their managers.

Even though they do not like the job, they continue with it because they do like the security. However, these individuals are likely to be looking for other types of work, just in case they can find something that they might like better.

Belonging

At this stage things are starting to change a bit. People like to feel as though they are part of a team and of something that might matter. When you can make employees feel this way, you have a better shot of truly drawing them into your company and making them a valuable part of the team. They want to know that you appreciate what they do. Ideally, you will have a team and company set up where this happens automatically.

When someone is entrenched on this level of the hierarchy, they feel as though they are engaged sometimes, although there might still be some days when they do not feel this way. They could also still have a desire to leave if they were to find something that they felt was better. Even though things are certainly better at this level, they are still not fully engaged. That starts in the next level.

Importance

Now, we come to the penultimate level of the pyramid. At this level, a person truly feels as if they are a part of the team and the organization in general. They tend to be proud that they are on the team and that they see themselves as an important part of the business, not just another person collecting a paycheck. They feel important while they are at work, and they feel as if they are achieving something while they are there.

Even though they might enjoy what they do and they feel as if they are contributing, that does not mean they will stay. They could still leave if the perfect offer happened to come along.

Self-Actualization

This is the final level of the pyramid in Maslow's Hierarchy, and it is seldom achieved. In fact, there are only about 15% of workers who reach this rare level. These are people who are trying to achieve everything they possibly can. They want to help and inspire others, and they love working for the company. They are looking for ways to improve and to advance in the company, and they truly feel that the company's needs are important.

What Can You Learn from This?

Why did we choose to include Maslow's Hierarchy in this book? It is to give you more insight into your own level of happiness at work and to help you understand just how important it is to truly engage all of those other people who are on your marketing team.

If you want to have employees who are happy, who are giving their all, and who are not constantly looking for another job, then you need to make sure they are engaged. You need to make sure they have a good and interesting place to work where they feel welcome, safe, and valuable. Do everything you can to engage those employees. Here are some tips that can help you from a managerial level.

Tips for Better Engagement

Take the time to learn more about the employees. Listen to them and learn about their interests, and talk to them occasionally and mention those things that they enjoy. Remember the names of their family. When you do things like this, they understand they are important to you and the rest of the team. It's little things like this that can help strengthen the bond of a team. If they have problems or concerns, you want to listen to those and take care of them as soon as possible. Do not simply dismiss their issues as not being important.

In addition, everyone who comes to your team needs to feel as if they know exactly what they are doing and why they are doing it. As we've mentioned, everyone needs to have a role and they need to know that role. In addition, they will need onboarding and training to make sure they are up to speed with all of the tools and

234

platforms they will be using. Remember, just because someone has been in marketing for several years, it does not mean they use the same equipment or platform that you have. Make sure everyone has the proper training.

Training is just a part of it, though. You also need to make sure you are developing your people. Look at Maslow's Hierarchy again. People want more from a company and they want the ability to advance. Develop the employees and help them to grow. It not only helps with employee engagement, but also with organizational success. When you have your training and development goals linked to your strategic goals, everyone wins.

When one of your employees does something special, make sure you recognize them. If one of the members of your team comes up with a stellar marketing idea that's outside of the box and that really wows the customers, make sure that employee, and not you, gets the credit for it. If you try to take the credit for everything your employees do, you will soon find that they are not giving very much at work. They are about the furthest from engaged they can get.

Encourage teamwork, as well. When you have a team that trusts one another, cares about one another and the job, they tend to want to put forward their best. Having a good team that has one another's back and that all get along with one another is one of the best ways to engage employees. When you are also able to create a fun workplace, you will find that they tend to be happy to come to work each day. That's saying a lot when you look around and start listening to how many people out there say they are miserable when they go to their jobs.

The environment that you create for your marketing team should be one that does not cause a fear of failing, or of anything else for that matter. The employees should not be afraid to come to work for any reason. If they are afraid of constantly getting yelled at by their boss for everything, they are going to be afraid to make changes and decisions on their own.

Finally, as much as you should want to be there for your employees, you also don't want to be there too much. This simply means that you do not want to hover or make employees nervous, and you never want to micromanage.

Engagement Really Does Help Make the Company Stronger

Engagement is essential if you want to have a good team that wants to make a difference for your company. If you have a team that just doesn't care and is only going through the motions, how much good do you feel they are really going to do your company? Take the tips we've discussed here and utilize Marlow's Hierarchy to help improve the engagement at your company. You might find that your peers also want to use these methods for their own departments, so feel free to share with them.

Digital Skills Report

We've mentioned it before, but it bears repeating here. Technology is essential when it comes to marketing today, and the digital world has taken over. Technology is not static either. It is always growing and changing, and that means you and everyone on your team needs to keep up with these changes. Still, the number of people who are in this field and who have the needed digital skills seems to be on the decline.

Reports have been conducted that have surveyed marketers to see what their perceived skill level was versus their actual skill level. Many thought they were very competent and that they knew what they were doing. However, the digital skills report from Digital Marketing Institute Limited found that the digital skills actual levels were lacking severely.

Smart Insights found the same thing when they ran their survey. For many companies, this means they need to start training their employees to improve their digital skills sooner rather than later. They need to make sure that part of the recruiting process ensures the candidates have the proper digital skills, too. Marketers also need to make sure they are then keeping up with all of the changes and updates that are brought to digital marketing.

The Smart Insights survey also found that around 60% of a marketer's time now was spent working on managing digital activities. Many of those who are in the field know that they need to bump up their skills – in fact, 32% have said that they want to develop their skills further. Almost the same percentage said that they are looking for a senior role in marketing that focused on the digital realm.

What Skills Are Important?

Marketers have said that they want to improve a range of digital skills. Some of the ones most commonly mentioned include digital strategy and integrated planning, mobile marketing, social media,

SEO, email marking, PPC, and customer data and analytics. By improving these skills, they know that it is bound to help them to improve their marketing prowess.

Some marketers may be willing to learn more on their own, while others might be waiting for their company to train them. Ideally, it will be a combination of these two things. The company should always be willing to help their marketers to improve their skills and to learn new digital marketing tools. However, if an employee truly wants to improve his or her skills, they should be willing to work on getting training on their own, as well.

Digital is not just the future. Digital is the here and now. Marketers need to continue to embrace it, as it has truly changed the entire world of marketing.

Notes

This has been the last step in your POINTS methodology. As you might have noticed we have made a strong emphasis on the importance of motivated talent to keep your strategy solid. This chapter should have served to map out the following items on your list:

- Who are your current team members associated with your digital marketing strategy?
- What recruiting needs do you have? How will you recruit?
- What organizational design model will you apply?
- Do you have a clear budget for talent? Technology? Training?

Sustainment

- Do you have a clear idea of the new vendors and partners required to make your strategy a success?
- How will you keep your team motivated and engaged?

Make sure you have a sustainment plan and budget in place before you start implementation.

Conclusion

We've come to the end of the book, but that does not mean it is the end of your journey or the end of your learning. Take the information from this book and use it when you are developing your own version of the POINTS Method to help with your marketing.

What Comes Next?

Your goal should be to create a marketing lifecycle, which proceeds through several stages, and which you are always trying to improve. You can break this down into several steps. We'll give you a simple breakdown of what it looks like below.

- Plan – Creating the roadmap.
- Reach – Building awareness and driving visitors toward your site.
- Interact – Improve the experience for the customer and the flow of the content you are creating.
- Convert – Create multichannel sales.
- Engage – Good engagement will help you to keep customers, and it will help to increase loyalty.

- Brand – The goal with branding is to create a stronger and even emotional connection.

- Governance – This step is all about managing the growth of the company.

Each of the elements in the list above will then have five different tiers or steps including the initial foray into the creation of the plan, the management, and then the defining phase, followed by the quantified phase and finally the optimized phase. Let's get a bit of a better look at what each of these means below.

- Initial – This is basic lifecycle marketing, which happens at the beginning stages of most businesses.

- Managed – During this stage, you are focusing on improving your lifecycle marketing thorough each of the elements listed above.

- Defined – During this stage, your plans, created from information that you've found in this book, are starting to come together.

- Quantified – Here, you will have gone on to start properly managing the lifecycle marketing.

- Optimized – At this final stage, you have optimized your marketing. Of course, there are always things that you can change and improve, so never settle for "good enough."

Keep these basics in mind when you are starting to create your plan, and you can develop your roadmap to success.

Keep Learning

This book has covered a substantial number of items, and as much as it has covered, there are always more items that could be discussed or deeper looks taken into certain aspects of marketing. You want to keep learning and to keep innovating and improving your marketing tactics to make sure they are working on your customers and potential customers.

This is a field that is always changing and evolving, just as we discussed way back at the start of the book. Continue learning and keep up with all the latest changes and the latest technology that could help your marketing efforts. Look for the pros, cons, and how you can use different tech, tools, and ideas to your advantage. This is the only way to stay ahead of the competition and to ensure the success of your company.

Start developing your plan today so you can improve your marketing prowess going forward.

Acronym Finder

Throughout the course of this book, we've used quite a few acronyms. By the time you've reached this section, it might be difficult to remember what all of them mean.

Here, you will find a quick and handy reference for all the various acronyms we've used in the book. You can refer to these pages when you want to refresh your memory and get the meaning of the acronyms you need quickly. Eventually, you will likely have them all memorized.

Acronyms

3Cs – Customer Corporation, Competitor

7Cs – Collecting, Clues, Connecting, Causation, Correlation, Compensation, and Concept

Agile PM – Agile Project Management

AHT – Average Handling Time

API – Application Programming Interface

ART – Average Response Time

ASP – Average Selling Price

B2B – Business to Business

B2C – Business to Customer/Consumer

BCG Matrix – Boston Consulting Group Matrix, created in the 1970s

C2C – Consumer to Consumer

COCA – Cost of Customer Acquisition

CPA – Cost per Acquisition or Cost per Action

CPC – Cost per Click

CPL – Cost per Lead

CPM – Cost Per Thousand Impressions

CLV – CLV stands for Customer Lifetime Value

CRM – Customer Relationship Management

CMS – Content Management System

CTR – Click-Through Rate

CVP – Customer Value Proposition

DAM – Digital Asset Management

DBE – Digital Business Ecosystems

Ecommerce – Electronic Commerce

EDI – Electronic Data Interchange

ERP – Enterprise Resource Planning

FCommerce – Facebook Commerce

FRT – First Response Time

FTC – Federal Trade Commission

FTE- Full Time Equivalent

H2H – Human to Human

HCI – Human-Computer Interaction

HCM – Human Centered Marketing

HLT – Human Language Technology

HT – Handling Time

HTML – Hypertext Markup Language

HTTP – Hypertext transfer protocol

IA – Information Architecture

IMC – Integrated Marketing Community

IOT – Internet of Things

IxD – Interaction Design

JDBC – Java Database Connectivity

KPI – Key Performance Indicators

LTV – Lifetime Value of a Customer

MBO – Management by Objectives

MCommerce – Mobile Commerce

MMS – Multimedia Messaging Service

MP – Market Potential

MQL – Marketing Qualified Lead

MS - Market Share (Percentage of Customers Buying from Your Company, Used in Formula for Determining MP)

N – Total Number of Potential Customers (Used in Formula for Determining MP)

.NET – Network

NLP – Natural Language Processing

NPS – Net Promoter Score

OKR – Objectives & Key Results

P – Average Selling Price (Used in Formula for Determining MP)

P2P – Peer to Peer

PM – Project Management

POINTS – People, Problem, Purpose, Partners, Objectives, Initiatives, Numbers Technology, Sustainability

PPC – Pay Per Click

PPL – Pay Per Lead

PPS – Pay Per Sale

ROI – Return on Investment

ROPO – Research Online, Purchase Offline

Q – Average Annual Consumption (Used in Formula for Determining MP)

SAP – Systems, Applications & Products in Data Processing

SEM – Search Engine Marketing

SEO – Search Engine Optimization

SERP – Search Engine Results Page

SMART Methodology – Specific, Measurable Achievable, Realistic, and Time-Based Methodology

SMS – Short Message Service

SOLOMO – Social, Local, and Mobile Marketing

SQL – Sales Qualified Lead

TAM – Total Available Market

THT – Total Handling Time

UI – User Interface

UX – User Experience

ZMOT – Zero Moment of Truth

WWW – World Wide Web

Resources

Image source lookout: www.sergiorestrepo.com/points

https://digitalmarketinginstitute.com/the-insider/05-10-16-the-evolution-of-digital-marketing-30-years-in-the-past-and-future

http://www.internetlivestats.com/internet-users/

http://www.yourarticlelibrary.com/marketing/evolution-of-market-segmentation-approaches-explained/22185/

http://www.business-fundas.com/2011/the-4-ps-of-marketing-the-marketing-mix-strategies/

https://hbr.org/2015/06/a-better-way-to-map-brand-strategy

http://learnmarketing.net/perceptualmaps.htm

http://customersthatstick.com/blog/customer-service-techniques/understanding-customer-lifetime-value-a-non-geek-guide/

http://www.businessdictionary.com/definition/market-segmentation.html

http://www.marketing91.com/6-advantages-segmentation/

https://blog.udemy.com/benefits-of-market-segmentation/

http://www.bcgmatrix.org/

https://www.nbea.org/newsite/curriculum/standards/marketing.html

https://www.ftc.gov/tips-advice/business-center/advertising-and-marketing

https://centermassmedia.com/the-basics-of-digital-marketing/

http://www.marketingprofs.com/articles/2014/26049/five-tips-and-examples-for-digital-marketing-success

https://www.thebalance.com/what-is-integrated-marketing-and-why-is-it-important-2295739

https://thedma.org/membership/member-groups-communities/integrated-marketing-community/integrated-marketing-definitions/

http://www.tronviggroup.com/marketing-strategy/

http://charliesaidthat.com/digital/digital/difference-between-marketing-strategy-vs-tactics-an-example/

http://www.streetdirectory.com/travel_guide/17636/marketing/what_is_a_marketing_initiative.html

http://viewpoints.io/entry/design-thinking-basics-five-simple-steps

https://www.marketingweek.com/2017/06/28/digital-transformation-new-challenges-how-to-overcome-them/

https://www.marketingweek.com/2016/04/14/what-does-digital-transformation-really-mean/

Resources

http://3gamma.com/insights/understanding-the-eight-drivers-of-digital-change/

https://thejournal.com/articles/2011/10/04/driving-digital-change.aspx

http://blog.seeburger.com/cloud-services-as-the-driver-of-digital-change-what-do-you-need-to-know/

https://www.forbes.com/forbes/welcome/?toURL=https://www.forbes.com/sites/forbesinsights/2017/01/03/5-steps-to-success-in-digital-transformation/&refURL=https://www.bing.com/&referrer=https://www.bing.com/

http://www.mckinsey.com/business-functions/digital-mckinsey/our-insights/digital-transformation-the-three-steps-to-success

http://susangarrettdogagility.com/2009/06/achieving-mastery/

https://www.forbes.com/sites/joemckendrick/2014/04/16/10-concrete-steps-to-take-on-the-road-to-digital-transformation-a-checklist/#160823a7350d

https://centricdigital.com/blog/digital-transformation/10-steps-to-guiding-a-companies-digital-transformation/

http://www.bryankramer.com/there-is-no-more-b2b-or-b2c-its-human-to-human-h2h/

http://tonyzambito.com/power-hcm-human-centered-marketing-begins-empathy/

http://www.marketingdive.com/news/does-values-based-marketing-really-work/409200/

http://www.buyerpersona.com/

http://tonyzambito.com/

https://university.custora.com/for-marketers/customer-centric-marketing/basic/what-is-customer-centric-marketing

http://www.businessinsider.com/the-critical-first-step-in-creating-a-successful-marketing-plan-2014-1

http://smallbusiness.chron.com/goals-valuesbased-marketing-21639.html

http://www.buyerpersona.com/what-is-a-buyer-persona

https://www.mymarketingdept.com/customer-centric-marketing

https://www.forbes.com/sites/danielnewman/2015/02/17/marketing-building-a-customer-centric-marketing-eco-system/#3aeab8b11cb2

https://university.custora.com/for-marketers/customer-centric-marketing/basic/the-benefits-of-customer-centric-marketing

http://www.the-future-of-commerce.com/2016/09/26/definition-consumer-journey/

https://www.hausmanmarketingletter.com/5-reasons-you-need-a-listening-post-to-enhance-your-social-media-marketing-strategy/

http://michaelrhunter.com/why-knowing-your-competition-is-important/

https://www.fastcompany.com/1838924/how-serial-innovators-find-best-problems-solve

Resources

http://www.customerexperienceinsight.com/solve-customer-problems-and-make-more-sales/

http://managementhelp.org/personalproductivity/problem-solving.htm

http://www.somacon.com/p254.php

http://www.practicalecommerce.com/danwilson-defining-purpose

https://7geese.com/the-difference-between-core-values-mission-and-vision-statements-and-goals/

https://www.powerlinx.com/resources/types-strategic-partnerships/

http://nonprofitinclusiveness.org/identifying-internal-and-external-stakeholders

https://www.boundless.com/accounting/textbooks/boundless-accounting-textbook/introduction-to-accounting-1/overview-of-key-elements-of-the-business-19/business-stakeholders-internal-and-external-117-6595/

https://www.econsultancy.com/blog/69182-a-complete-guide-to-partnership-marketing-part-one

https://www.econsultancy.com/blog/69190-a-complete-guide-to-partnership-marketing-part-two/

https://weekdone.com/resources/objectives-key-results

http://www.thedsmgroup.com/your-guide-company-objectives-key-results/

http://www.techrepublic.com/article/use-smart-goals-to-launch-management-by-objectives-plan/

http://www.yourcoach.be/en/coaching-tools/smart-goal-setting.php

http://www.wikihow.com/Set-SMART-Goals

http://www.smart-goals-guide.com/smart-goal-setting.html

http://www.self-esteem-enhances-life.com/measurable-goals.html

http://work.chron.com/important-set-measurable-goals-supervisor-20694.html

https://www.mindtools.com/pages/article/newHTE_90.htm

http://smallbusiness.chron.com/set-challenging-goals-71865.html

https://www.entrepreneur.com/article/57270

https://plantsforhumanhealth.ncsu.edu/extension/marketready/pdfs-ppt/business_development_files/PDF/estimating_market_potential.pdf

http://www.successdesigns.net/articles/entry/how-to-define-your-target-market/

http://study.com/academy/lesson/what-is-competition-in-marketing-definition-types-quiz.html

http://sherpablog.marketingsherpa.com/marketing/competition-types-to-watch/

http://www.marketingprofs.com/Tutorials/marketsize1.asp

Resources

http://smallbusiness.chron.com/tips-defining-size-market-startup-business-593.html

http://blog.marketresearch.com/5-steps-to-estimate-market-size

https://www.fool.com/knowledge-center/average-selling-price.aspx

http://www.investopedia.com/terms/a/averagesellingprice.asp

http://www.investopedia.com/terms/p/product-life-cycle.asp

http://www.investopedia.com/terms/f/forecasting.asp

http://smallbusiness.chron.com/market-demand-market-potential-sales-forecasting-related-other-1485.html

https://www.inc.com/guides/201109/how-to-assess-the-market-potential-of-your-new-business-idea.html

http://smallbusiness.chron.com/calculate-fte-742.html

http://www.joanmcarthurtraining.com/workshops-coaching-consulting/collaborative-ideation/

https://www.stlouisfed.org/Publications/Bridges/Summer-2009/The-Four-Key-Elements-of-Innovation-Collaboration-Ideation-Implementation-and-Value-Creation

https://www.thoughtfarmer.com/blog/good-collaboration-10-tips/

http://www.innovationmanagement.se/2013/05/30/the-7-all-time-greatest-ideation-techniques/

http://www.vincegowmon.com/7-mindsets-for-collaboration/

http://www.gartner.com/technology/topics/business-ecosystems.jsp

https://brilliantnoise.com/blog/the-digital-ecosystem/

http://www.cio.com/article/2878419/innovation/how-digital-ecosystems-are-creating-the-we-economy.html

http://ydc2.yale.edu/digital-ecosystem

https://www.forbes.com/sites/ciocentral/2015/03/09/the-rise-of-digital-ecosystems-in-the-we-economy/#6439ab405514

https://www.forbes.com/sites/danielnewman/2014/12/03/the-role-of-paid-owned-and-earned-media-in-your-marketing-strategy/#482c5f6528bf

https://smallbiztrends.com/2013/08/what-is-owned-earned-paid-media.html

http://www.huffingtonpost.com/john-lusk/how-to-define-and-use-pai_b_4634005.html

https://www.titan-seo.com/NewsArticles/trifecta.html

https://www.brandwatch.com/blog/define-measure-paid-owned-earned-media/

https://blog.hootsuite.com/converged-media-brito-part-1/

http://mediakix.com/2016/09/paid-owned-earned-media-difference-definition/

https://www.dreamgrow.com/top-15-most-popular-social-networking-sites/

Resources

https://blog.hootsuite.com/18-social-media-marketing-tips/

https://www.postplanner.com/top-10-mistakes-businesses-make-on-social-media/

https://blog.hootsuite.com/how-to-create-a-social-media-marketing-plan/

https://hootsuite.com/resources/guide/top-10-social-media-tips-for-small-businesses

https://sproutsocial.com/insights/social-media-tips/

https://www.thoughtworks.com/agile-project-management

http://www.dummies.com/careers/project-management/agile-project-management-for-dummies-cheat-sheet/

http://observer.com/2017/08/social-media-legal-trouble-copyright-law/

http://blog.capterra.com/5-ways-to-teach-agile-methodology-to-your-tech-team/

http://blog.capterra.com/agile-project-management-software/

http://searchmanufacturingerp.techtarget.com/definition/Rapid-prototyping

https://www.usertesting.com/blog/2015/09/16/what-is-ux-design-15-user-experience-experts-weigh-in/

https://careerfoundry.com/en/blog/ux-design/the-difference-between-ux-and-ui-design-a-laymans-guide/

https://www.usability.gov/what-and-why/user-experience.html

http://uxdesign.com/assets/Elements-of-User-Experience.pdf

http://usabilitygeek.com/user-experience/

https://www.smashingmagazine.com/2010/10/what-is-user-experience-design-overview-tools-and-resources/

https://www.usability.gov/what-and-why/user-interface-design.html

https://www.forbes.com/sites/joshsteimle/2014/09/19/what-is-content-marketing/#6f3ab3fb10b9

http://www.cision.com/us/2015/11/5-must-have-types-of-content-marketing/

http://contentmarketinginstitute.com/2016/06/content-crave-infographic/

https://www.singlegrain.com/blog-posts/content-marketing/content-marketing-funnel-using-different-types-content/

https://www.forbes.com/sites/sujanpatel/2016/03/24/25-content-marketing-tips-every-marketer-needs-to-know/#52172fa226d3

https://www.salesforce.com/blog/2012/06/blog-seo-tips-how-to-seo-your-blog.html

https://www.bloggertipstricks.com/on-page-seo-tips-blogspot.html

http://www.blogtyrant.com/beginner-blogging-seo/

https://blogging.org/blog/simple-seo-tips-bloggers/

http://www.socialmediaexaminer.com/12-types-of-blog-posts/

Resources

http://www.cio.com/article/2867406/marketing/how-to-use-ebooks-to-improve-your-content-marketing-strategy.html

http://www.copyblogger.com/ebook-marketing/

https://www.scribd.com/document/100565166/Using-eBooks-in-Content-Marketing

http://labs.openviewpartners.com/ebook-tips/

http://www.rightmixmarketing.com/content-marketing/ebooks-for-content-marketing/

https://digitalmarketinginstitute.com/blog/2017-5-19-3-ways-use-ebooks-content-marketing-strategy1

http://www.convinceandconvert.com/content-marketing/infographic-marketing/

https://marketinginsidergroup.com/content-marketing/7-tips-building-trust-content-marketing/

http://www.socialmediaexaminer.com/proof-that-podcasting-will-benefit-your-business/

http://www.bitrebels.com/design/8-types-of-infographics-use-when/

http://www.podcasting-tools.com/10-tips-podcasting.htm

http://mashable.com/2011/03/25/podcasting-tips/

http://www.themarketingagents.com/expert-podcasting-tips

http://www.socialmediaexaminer.com/6-podcasting-tips-from-the-pros/

https://www.entrepreneur.com/article/243024

https://www.entrepreneurs-journey.com/1039/the-7-secrets-to-a-successful-podcast/

http://contentmarketinginstitute.com/2015/10/use-video-content-marketing/

https://www.entrepreneur.com/article/243208

http://contentmarketinginstitute.com/2013/03/video-content-marketing-effective-strategy/

http://www.curata.com/blog/video-content-marketing/

https://www.theguardian.com/small-business-network/2014/jan/14/video-content-marketing-media-online

https://www.marketingprofs.com/articles/2017/32342/how-to-use-video-to-achieve-your-marketing-goals-from-awareness-to-sales-and-in-between

https://www.marketingprofs.com/articles/2017/31476/how-to-use-video-content-to-create-a-loyal-audience

https://www.forbes.com/sites/johnrampton/2015/02/04/5-things-your-video-marketing-strategy-should-include/#139379ae12a3

https://www.ftc.gov/news-events/press-releases/2017/04/ftc-staff-reminds-influencers-brands-clearly-disclose

https://www.ftc.gov/tips-advice/business-center/guidance/ftcs-endorsement-guides-what-people-are-asking

https://www.hubspot.com/inbound-marketing

https://www.sideqik.com/together-marketing/10-benefits-of-influencer-marketing

https://blog.hubspot.com/blog/tabid/6307/bid/28330/23-Reasons-Inbound-Marketing-Trumps-Outbound-Marketing-Infographic.aspx

http://www.business2community.com/inbound-marketing/5-key-benefits-inbound-marketing-01241334#dMdiIyRHLjZ0KJk9.97

https://www.forbes.com/sites/ajagrawal/2016/01/21/why-inbound-marketing-is-essential-in-2016/#3b0643a86554

https://www.forbes.com/sites/ajagrawal/2016/01/21/why-inbound-marketing-is-essential-in-2016/#3b0643a86554

https://blog.hubspot.com/insiders/what-is-marketing-automation-a-beginners-guide?_ga=2.268898232.850884623.1502315312-1042301346.1501726320

https://smallbiztrends.com/2017/05/automated-marketing-small-business.html

http://www.capterra.com/marketing-automation-software/

https://www.quicksprout.com/the-definitive-guide-to-marketing-automation-chapter-1/

https://www.simplycast.com/blog/top-10-benefits-of-marketing-automation/

https://blog.hubspot.com/insiders/marketing-automation-facts

http://www.networksolutions.com/education/what-is-ecommerce/

http://www.paymentgateways.org.in/

https://www.brainsins.com/en/blog/top-10-payment-gateways-e-commerce-us/3661

http://blog.sumall.com/journal/10-best-practices-improve-e-commerce-website.html

http://tweakyourbiz.com/technology/2016/03/02/5-tips-improve-mobile-website-commerce/

http://marketingland.com/mobile-commerce-5-ways-company-can-improve-155746

https://www.techopedia.com/definition/28577/facebook-commerce-f-commerce

http://mashable.com/2011/07/14/facebook-commerce-guide/#qnrf8KxlNkqo

http://www.cj.com/what-is-affiliate-marketing

http://www.wisegeek.org/what-is-affiliate-marketing.htm

https://gowide.com/news/-irresistible-benefits-of-pay-per-lead-marketing-model

https://www.forbes.com/sites/steveolenski/2014/07/08/4-myths-about-affiliate-marketing-you-need-to-know/2/#411c80e37f20

https://chexxinc.com/3-affiliate-marketing-myths/

https://medialeaders.com/marketing-augmented-reality-dgs6/

http://www.socialmediatoday.com/content/5-benefits-augmented-reality-marketing

Resources

http://www.ikea.com/ca/en/about_ikea/newsitem/2014catalogue

http://www.webopedia.com/TERM/I/internet_of_things.html

https://www.forbes.com/sites/neilpatel/2015/12/10/how-the-internet-of-things-is-changing-online-marketing/#7f99a09b6880

https://www.salesforce.com/blog/2014/03/internet-of-things-marketing-impact.html

https://www.forbes.com/sites/johnrampton/2015/09/28/driving-customer-engagement-through-an-interactive-and-gamified-environment/#1d064f9678bc

https://elearningindustry.com/6-practices-5-features-gamified-learning-environment

https://www.inc.com/guide/2010/06/picking-effective-seo-keywords.html

http://searchengineland.com/guide/seo/site-architecture-search-engine-ranking

https://www.searchenginejournal.com/bad-seo-techniques-that-will-hurt-your-google-rankings/7065/

http://www.intranetconnections.com/blog/4-essentials-for-your-marketing-intranet/

https://www.salesforce.com/blog/2013/01/what-is-crm-your-business-nerve-center.html

https://www.impactbnd.com/blog/crm-software

https://www.forbes.com/sites/aileron/2013/05/01/why-your-small-business-needs-crm/#6b6e7e316008

http://www.toptenreviews.com/business/software/best-crm-software/

http://www.businessnewsdaily.com/7839-best-crm-software.html

http://www.enterpriseappstoday.com/crm/8-common-crm-mistakes-and-how-to-avoid-them.html

http://www.cio.com/article/2390144/customer-relationship-management/10-crm-mistakes-and-how-you-can-avoid-making-them.html

https://emailmarketing.comm100.com/email-marketing-ebook/email-marketing-benefits.aspx

https://www.ventureharbour.com/email-marketing-software-tools-one-best/

https://blog.hubspot.com/blog/tabid/6307/bid/30718/15-Tenets-of-Proper-Email-Marketing-Etiquette.aspx

https://www.sas.com/en_us/insights/marketing/marketing-analytics.html

https://www.sas.com/en_us/insights/analytics/predictive-analytics.html

http://www.demandgenreport.com/industry-topics/demanding-views/2257-small-data-vs-big-data-whats-better-in-marketing-.html

https://www.bbvaopenmind.com/en/small-data-vs-big-data-back-to-the-basics/

Resources

http://www.marketingprofs.com/opinions/2016/30899/
predictive-analysis-the-action-is-in-the-small-data

http://whatis.techtarget.com/definition/small-data

https://www.entrepreneur.com/article/227957

http://www.doz.com/analytics/10-top-online-marketing-
platforms

https://www.entrepreneur.com/article/240030

https://www.g2crowd.com/categories/marketing-automation

https://www.forbes.com/sites/groupthink/2013/09/24/6-things-
online-retailers-can-learn-from-amazon/#7c9bf8dc237b

http://www.practicalecommerce.com/5-Tips-for-Increasing-
Amazon-Sales-by-50-Percent

https://www.forbes.com/sites/groupthink/2013/09/24/6-things-
online-retailers-can-learn-from-amazon/#7c9bf8dc237b

http://mashable.com/2011/04/15/ebay-
marketing/#h7OKYf6GISqo

https://www.entrepreneur.com/article/84176

http://projects.wsj.com/alibaba/

http://searchengineland.com/guide/what-is-sem

http://searchengineland.com/guide/what-is-paid-search

http://www.webopedia.com/TERM/E/ecommerce_remarketing.
html

https://econsultancy.com/blog/66207-how-can-nlp-technology-be-used-for-marketing/

http://www.cision.com/us/2013/01/what-is-solomo-and-why-is-it-important-to-marketers/

http://www.cio.com/article/2381406/marketing/10-mobile-marketing-tips-for-small-businesses.html

http://adsolutions.yp.com/engage-on-social-media/social-local-mobile

https://blogs.mulesoft.com/dev/api-dev/series-apis-connectors-integration-applications/

http://www.toolpack.com/charting.html

http://smallbusiness.chron.com/marketing-department-organizational-structure-716.html

https://www.ragan.com/Main/Articles/The_top_20_alternatives_to_SharePoint_45308.aspx

https://www.entrepreneur.com/article/243790

https://vtldesign.com/digital-marketing/content-marketing-strategy/percent-of-revenue-spent-on-marketing-sales/

http://frog-dog.com/how-much-should-companies-budget-for-marketing/

https://www.thebalance.com/vendor-management-success-tips-2533810

http://www.loyaltyworks.com/news-and-views/uncategorized/maslows-hierarchy-of-needs-and-employee-engagement/

Resources

https://www.entrepreneur.com/article/244978

https://www.sparkreaction.com/blog/buyers-journey-vs-customer-lifecycle

https://medium.customerlabs.co/saas-demystifying-customer-lifecycle-and-customer-journeys-fa078ad482e6

http://dmresourcecenter.com/unit-3/geofencing/

https://digitalassetmanagement.com/

POINTS METHODOLOGY